THE SEARCH FOR ENERGY

NO GAS

GASOLINE
BY
APPOINTMENT
ONLY

NO
GAS

Due to limited sup

SORRY...
NO
GASOLINE
TODAY

THE SEARCH FOR ENERGY

By Don Dwiggins

Illustrated with Photographs and Diagrams

A GOLDEN GATE JUNIOR BOOK

Childrens Press, Chicago

ACKNOWLEDGEMENTS

THE SEARCH For Energy began for the author in the long lines at the corner gas station, wondering how in the world we had gotten ourselves into such a mess, and how we were going to get out of it. As the story unfolded, the overall picture became quite different. Its perspective reached back to the beginnings of time, across the cosmos, and back once more to the corner gas station, as I sought to define the sources of energy that keep our technological society humming.

Many prior energy crises stood revealed as man depleted one resource after another—firewood, whale oil, and now our diminishing supplies of fossil fuels. Already, as we enter the Age of Atomic Energy, the end of our uranium supplies is in sight, and so we finally turn to alternative energy sources, from direct solar power to nuclear fusion, still hoping to stay out of those long lines at future gas stations.

I have been helped in this research by many people and organizations, including the Atomic Energy Commission, the American Oil Institute, the Livermore Radiation Laboratory, Dr. Robert W. Rex, president of Republic Geothermal, Incorporated, the UCLA Research Library staff, Pacific Gas & Electric Company, Princeton University's Plasma Physics Laboratory, Southern California Edision Company, and Southern California Gas Company. Thanks also go to Dr. William M. Hooke and to my editor, Marjorie Thayer, for their careful editing.

DON DWIGGINS

Library of Congress Cataloging in Publication Data

Dwiggins, Don.
  The search for energy.

  SUMMARY: Discusses the discovery of different forms of energy, their uses in the past, and the possibilities for new kinds of energy in the future.
  "A Golden Gate junior book."
  1. Power resources—Juvenile literature.
[1. Power resources. 2. Force and energy] I. Title.
TJ153.D88   333.7   74-7407
ISBN 0-516-08857-2

CONTENTS

FOREWORD

THROUGH THE years energy has been transmitted silently and invisibly into our homes and schools, and we have used it with little consideration of its origins or the implications of its consumption. We have been almost unaware of energy because it is not an ordinary, simple commodity we can hold in our hands. Rather, energy is the name we give for a capability; a capability for doing work. And very recently our society has become aware of its absolute dependence on energy. A decrease in a small fraction of our energy supply is justifiably termed a crisis. Energy crises will come and go, and they will be greatly affected by political forces, but the fundamental problem of inadequate energy sources will persist and slowly intensify in the coming decades. The solutions to this problem involve countless choices and decisions by governments and individuals. The little decisions we make every day as we choose our transportation, adjust a thermostat, or flick a light switch, represent, in effect, votes for an energy policy. And so the need for us to learn the essentials of this fascinating field is similar to the need for a politically aware electorate in a democracy.

A growing army of government officials, scientists, engineers and environmentalists is directing its efforts to the solutions of these problems. As an example, along with workers in several other laboratories in this country and throughout the world, we at the Princeton Plasma Physics Laboratory are working toward the eventual achievement of controlled thermonuclear fusion. We believe that, if this goal is reached, we will be tapping an energy source which possesses the ultimate combination of fuel availability, safety and freedom from air pollution. If this sounds exciting but somewhat unintelligible, then I refer you to a clear, concise account of the field of fusion energy in this book. In fact, Don Dwiggins has, in this book, written an excellent and vivid description of the wide-ranging activities associated with the search for energy. Indeed, this work represents a step toward the goal of an informed "energy electorate."

WILLIAM M. HOOKE
Associate Head, Experimental Division
Princeton Plasma Physics Laboratory

Arabian Peninsula

IS THE WORLD RUNNING OUT OF GAS?

EXPLODING ACROSS the land with the shock wave of an atomic bomb, the worldwide energy crisis of 1973-74 caught millions of people unawares. Despite ample warnings that a fuel crisis was long overdue, few people accepted the seriousness of the matter. It took the Middle East War of October, 1973, to get the message through—the world was running out of gas. The bad news focused attention on Saudi Arabia, a nation that owns a quarter of the entire world's proved oil reserves.

Within the walled city of Riyadh, Saudi Arabia's King Faisal issued embargo orders, cutting off oil shipments to much of the world. Amidst the confusion that followed, people reacted with anger and frustration, blaming their governments, the big oil companies, and each other for the mess they found themselves in.

In the United States, as in other countries, certain facts stood out. For too long we had run our cars, heated and lighted our homes, and run our factories on precious, limited supplies of fossil fuels—the natural gas, oil, coal, and shale deposits stored in the Earth over hundreds of millions of years.

Gigantic underwater petroleum storage tank, the first of its kind, is towed by ocean-going tugs to a site off Dubai in Arabian Gulf, where it was submerged in 1969 to await transfer of crude oil to tankers for worldwide delivery.

The answer to the problem was plain—the world must eventually turn to other energy sources and lock up this planet's remaining fossil fuels in a treasure vault marked *For Emergency Use Only!* In this country the transition already had begun, with introduction of nuclear power plants in the 1960's, but not until the twenty-first century could we expect a major shift to atomic power.

In the meantime we could do two things—reduce our total energy consumption, and develop as a stopgap such other energy sources as the heat locked up inside the Earth in the form of geothermal energy, the energy of the winds and the tides, the radiant energy in sunlight itself.

As a first step in understanding the long-range crisis, it is necessary to form a clear picture of just what energy is, and how it can best be utilized in our everyday lives. A modern technological society, such as we have in the United States, runs like a huge machine. This machine must operate at a high level of efficiency to keep functioning properly, and it must have an adequate energy input—its fuel.

Our technological machine runs according to two fundamental rules, called Laws of Thermodynamics. The first of these two laws says energy can neither be created nor destroyed, although it can change from one form to another, such as the energy of motion (kinetic energy), potential energy (gravitational), chemical energy, heat energy, nuclear energy, and energy associated with mass itself, expressed in 1905 by Dr. Albert Einstein, a brilliant, twenty-six-year-old theoretical physicist, in his classic formula: $E = mc^2$.

Huge oil tankers like the Universe Iran *provide transportation of petroleum to an oil-hungry world. Oil embargo imposed by King Faisal of Saudi Arabia precipitated a global crisis that prompted renewed search for other energy sources.*

The second law of thermodynamics says, in effect, that heat (energy) must flow from hot to cold to do work. While the amount of energy in the universe remains constant, according to the first law, the second law says the amount of energy available to do work constantly diminishes. At some point, then, the total energy of the universe will be changed, through various forms, to an ultimate state of inert uniformity. We call this *entropy,* from the Greek word for *change.*

There can be no such thing as a perfectly efficient machine—there is always some energy loss, even in complete absence of friction. Over the centuries brilliant minds have conceived perpetual motion machines supposed to run with 100 percent efficiency, but none has ever worked. About the closest we come to an energy transfer without loss is in harnessing the gravitational energy of falling water, in a hydroelectric power station, to produce electricity.

Fossil fuels in the long run have far more value as an energy source for transportation, heating and lighting, all of which can get along on different kinds of power. More important, perhaps, is their use as a source of ammonia for nitrogen fertilizers to increase the world's food supply for our exploding population. Fossil fuels also serve as feedstock for our massive petrochemical industry, in the manufacture of plastic goods, synthetic cloths and rubber tires, and other such products on which our technological society depends.

A look back across the pages of time shows that the energy crisis was to be expected; in the past thirty years we have consumed more fossil

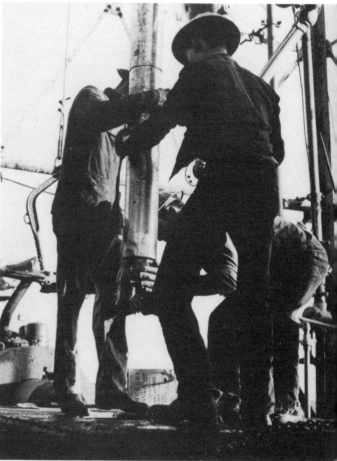

Billionaire Howard Hughes' fortune was built on invention of rock bit that made possible recovery of oil from deep deposits of fossil fuels—"stored sunshine".

Signal Hill, in Long Beach, California, world's richest oil field in barrels per acre, is a forest of derricks due to early subdivision of the land into building lots.

fuels than in *all previous history.* By 1970, 95.9 percent of our total consumed energy came from this single source.

As the United States became a mobilized society, the demand for automotive fuel outstripped the supply. Although the Middle East actually furnishes only a small percentage of our petroleum needs, at our current rate of consumption the United States will have to import *50 percent* of its oil and gas within the next decade, unless we tap other energy sources.

This is a conclusion of the Congressional Joint Committee on Atomic Energy, which warned in 1973 that we were already "in the twilight of the fossil age." The Joint Committee further suggested that the only way we can make the transition to other energy sources is through buying time with an accelerated use of our remaining domestic fossil fuel resources, and by

Offshore drilling rigs like this have opened vast new areas for oil recovery from deposits below continental shelf zones, both along coastlines of North America and other continents.

Escaping natural gas can cause oil well fire disasters that sometimes rage for months or years before being brought under control. Oil and gas exist together in deep reserves.

energy conservation.

A search for new fossil fuel deposits was spurred by an earlier Arab-Israeli War in 1967, when the vital Suez Canal and two huge oil pipelines were cut. While the United States is not as dependent as are Europe and the Far East on Saudi Arabian oil, the danger was apparent. Beyond the continental limits of the United States oil exploration was stepped up, and within a year of the 1967 Middle East conflict, the Prudhoe Bay strike on Alaska's North Slope turned out to be the biggest oil discovery in the western hemisphere. Offshore oil drilling in the Gulf of Mexico, and off Santa Barbara, California, increased dramatically. Leases went for as much as $600 million, highest on record.

Such exploratory efforts were frequently viewed as outright greed,

Modern oil fields in the United States are planned for maximum recovery of petroleum with minimum number of widely spaced wells, while many natural gas fields have only one well per 640 acres.

not necessity. Opposition mounted from concerned environmentalists, sickened by what they saw as the rape of our land. Not only oil spills in the Santa Barbara Channel, and the threat of similar pollution in Alaska, should a proposed oil pipeline from the North Slope to Valdez rupture, but other despoiling was feared. Was it better to have more and more cheap gas for weekend pleasure driving, our environmentalist asked, or a world of natural beauty to visit?

Of major concern was the lifting of restrictions on public lands by the Department of the Interior to permit strip-mining of coal, uranium, and oil shale. Similar concern was expressed over proposed drilling of deep wells to tap the heat energy inside the Earth for geothermal power.

Perhaps the loudest cries were raised against the proliferation of nuclear fission power plants, through unreasonable fear of an accidental atomic explosion, concern over the disposal or potential release of radioactive waste, and of thermal pollution by discharge of water used to cool the nuclear piles. The controversy was short-sighted — actually, well-designed

Modern oil refineries and cracking towers form the basis for the giant petrochemical industry, supplying not only gasoline for automobiles and aircraft and diesel fuel for trucks, but feed stocks for the giant plastics industry and for fertilizers.

nuclear power stations offer the cleanest, most efficient solution to the growing energy crisis. By January 1, 1974, a total of 39 atomic energy plants were operating within the United States, a number expected to grow to 650 by the year 2,000.

The final straw, to conservationists, was a proposal to dam the Colorado River in the Grand Canyon, and turn that natural wonder into a huge hydroelectric power storage basin. There had to be another way to solve the energy crisis, and there was — through the atom.

Once we make the transition from fossil to nuclear fuels, perhaps in the next quarter-century, our technological machine should be in fairly good running order. Perhaps the energy crisis of 1973-74 came at just the right time, to make us aware of what we have been doing to "Spaceship Earth" — our own solitary planet in the vastness of the Universe.

But first we must understand how energy works, and where man's eternal search for power has taken him through the centuries. By knowing the past, we can get a clearer picture of our energy future.

In 1883 Thomas Edison discovered the basis for modern electron tubes, by placing a small metal plate between legs of a filament to control current, the Edison Effect.

MAN'S ETERNAL SEARCH FOR POWER

What's past is prologue.
— William Shakespeare.

OF ALL the forms of energy in use today, electricity is one of the most familiar, though it's been less than one hundred years since it was first used for lighting. On October 20, 1878, Thomas Alva Edison lit history's first electric light bulb by passing a current through a filament of carbonized cellulose fiber. It burned for 13½ hours. Today we take such a miracle for granted, and perhaps overlook the fact that more than half of all the coal mined in this country today is used to generate electricity.

Pause a moment. As you read this page, perhaps in the friendly glow of an electric lamp, do you really know *where* the light comes from?

Like all energy on Earth (except, perhaps, nuclear and geothermal), it

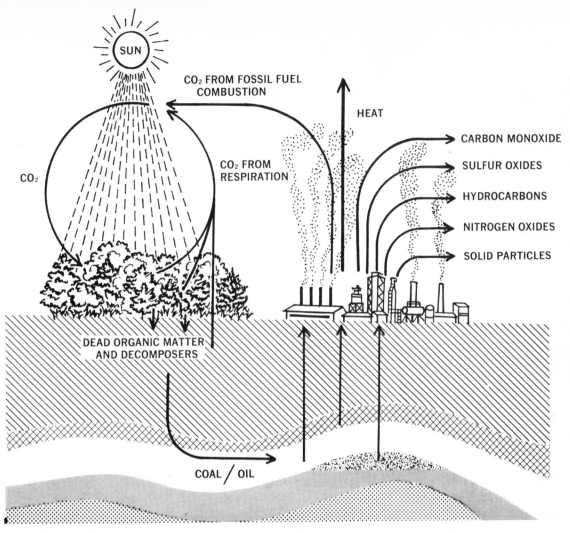

Our world's total energy system is made up of vast number of systems which play mutually supportive roles. Of greatest interest in relation to fossil fuels is the carbon cycle, above, in which energy from the Sun is stored in Spaceship Earth for recycling.

begins as radiant energy from the Sun. Solar energy, stored in fossil fuels through the miracle of photosynthesis, becomes chemical energy, which is released by combustion (heat energy), to turn water into steam to run turbines (mechanical energy) to turn electric generators (electromagnetic energy), to complete the circle by making light (radiant energy).

In a similar conversion, solar heat plays a primary role in the hydrology energy cycle — by the evaporation of ocean water that returns to Earth as rainfall, flowing down in mountain streams and spilling over dams to turn turbogenerators to make electricity, much in the same way the potential energy in falling water once turned waterwheels to produce mechanical (kinetic) energy.

Long-distance transmission of electricity, from hydroelectric or steam electric plants, did not come about until the 1920's when introduction of alternating current theory and booster stations made possible its distribution along transmission lines for distances of more than 200 miles.

THE WATER CYCLE

75% FALLS ON OCEANS

7% BLOWS OVER LAND

18% EVAPORATES FROM LAND

25% FALLS ON LAND

82% EVAPORATES FROM OCEANS

7% RUN OFF

SOIL MOISTURE

SEEPAGE

WATER TABLE

LAND-WATER DISTRIBUTION
RIVERS AND STREAMS... 00.014%
FRESH-WATER LAKES... 01.4
SALT LAKES AND
INLAND SEAS............. 01.2
SOIL MOISTURE
AND SEEPAGE........... 00.7
GROUND WATER
½ MILE DEEP 48.3
GROUND WATER
BELOW ½ MILE 48.3

A water crisis far more serious than the petroleum crisis would have world-shaking impact, except for a careful conservation program initiated seven decades ago by what is now the United States Bureau of Reclamation. Our exploding population has created a demand for more food, more electricity, more drinking and washing water, more water for industry, and more water for recreation. Of the world's top five major hydroelectric generating plants, two are in South America (Itaipu, Brazil-Paraguay, 10,710 megawatts, and Guri, Venezuela, 6,500 MW); two are in Russia (Sayansk, 6,400 MW, and Krasnoyarsk, 6,096 MW); and one in the United States (Grand Coulee, 9,780 MW ultimate capacity).

We can store electric energy in batteries of storage cells in limited quantities, but, generally speaking, electricity is one form of energy that is produced on demand, at the instant needed. One imaginative way of gearing hydroelectric power to periodic demand for electricity is in use today at Arizona's Salt River Valley Power Project. From midnight to sunrise, a time period when demand for electricity is minimal, water is pumped "uphill," from lower to higher storage basins, behind Horse Mesa and Mormon Flat Dams. The pumping is done by turbines that run the other way in the daytime, when the same water, flowing downhill, turns generators to supply electricity to the Valley. The next evening the generators, supplied with power from other sources, act as motors to turn the turbines to lift the water back uphill. Called the pump-back system, this arrangement operates with an overall efficiency of about 70 percent, twice that of a thermoelecric power plant burning fossil fuel for energy.

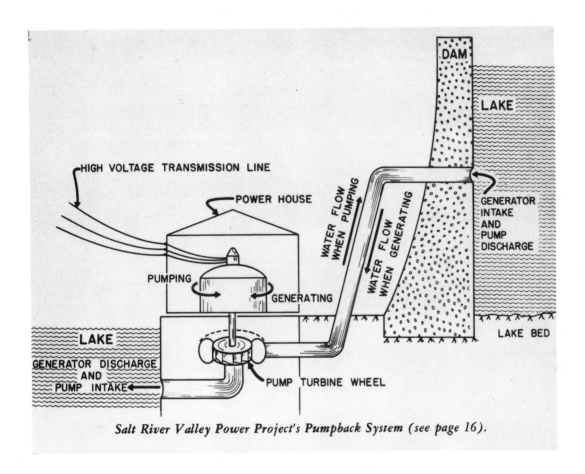

Salt River Valley Power Project's Pumpback System (see page 16).

People once thought electricity was a kind of fluid that flowed like water into one end of a copper wire and out the other. Benjamin Franklin, who held to this theory, believed there were two kinds of electrical charges; he named these *positive* and *negative.* The idea wasn't new — it dates back to Ancient Greece. A piece of amber, vigorously rubbed, attracts small particles of dust, and the Greeks had a word for it — *elektron,* for amber.

Today the atomic theory has replaced the fluid theory of electricity. We still refer to an electric "current," but the term is misleading. As we know, an atom is made up of a positively charged nucleus surrounded by negatively charged electrons. Normally, the sum of negative and positive charges is the same, and the atom is electrically neutral.

In some substances, like copper or silver, electrons are more loosely bound to their atomic nuclei than in others. Under certain conditions, these loosely bound electrons detach themselves from one atom and

Arizona's Mormon Flat Dam project uses pumpback system.

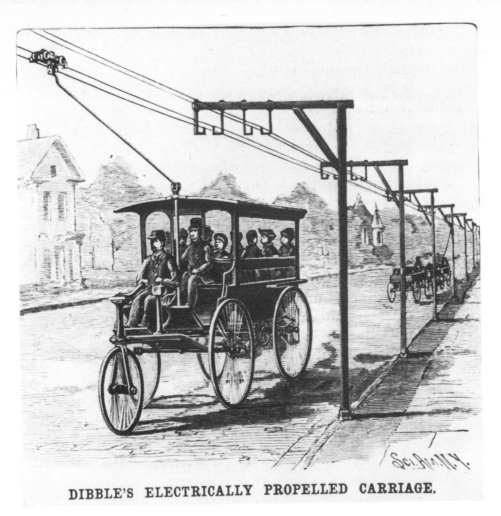

DIBBLE'S ELECTRICALLY PROPELLED CARRIAGE.

Rapid transit circa 1890 wasn't very rapid.

attach to another, leaving the first atom positively charged. Like water seeking its own level, electricity seeks to become neutral again, "flowing" from positive to negative. The electrons which make up the "current" are passed along from atom to atom, according to the difference in polarity, called *voltage.* The amount of flow is called *amperage,* the number of electrons that are passed from atom to atom in a conductor such as a copper wire. In a single second, one ampere of current will transfer 6,242,000,000,000,000,000 electrons through a single atom!

A generator creates an electric current by turning a coil of wire inside a magnetic field, producing pulses of positive charges. An electric motor is simply a generator in reverse; a current from the generator creates a magnetic field in a coil of wire called an armature, driven by other magnets around it that alternately "push and pull" it with positive and negative charges. An electric motor operates with high efficiency — more than 90 percent of the energy reaching it is converted into work.

In 1924 Los Angeles had 1,163 miles of rapid-transit steel railways with as many as 6,000 "big red cars" operating daily. In the period between 1932 and 1956, more than one hundred such electric rapid-transit surface systems throughout the United States were abandoned in favor of automobile freeway systems. Among the affected cities were Los Angeles, Baltimore, Philadelphia, New York, and St. Louis. Today, the nation faces the prospect of spending billions of dollars to bring back urban transit systems such as the old high-speed streetcars.

Electricity works for us in other ways. Some materials are poor conductors of electricity, due to what is called their *resistance;* if their atoms can't pass electrons along fast enough, the energy is converted into heat. Such a material is nickel-chromium alloy, of which heating elements in electric toasters, coffee pots, and other household appliances are made. The greater the resistance the more heat is developed, through a kind of friction within the atoms. Resistance is measured in *ohms,* named for George Ohm, who discovered the phenomenon.

Hydroelectric generators supply about ten percent of our total electric energy. Tidal power, wind power, solar power, and geothermal power are sometimes used on a small scale, but the major source of electricity is heat from fossil fuels.

Before the discovery of electricity, man used more direct energy conversion systems to supply his basic needs — food, heat, light, and mobility. At first he used muscle power alone, then he invented ways to make his

In medieval times man learned to harness the energy of gravity in flowing rivers to run watermills (left) and to operate pumps with undershot waterwheels (right), highly efficient systems.

work easier, with levers, wheels, pulleys, and other mechanisms.

In medieval Europe, water wheels harnessed rivers to grind corn. When the rivers ran dry, man turned to wind-powered mills, not only to grind corn, but to raise water with Archimedean screws and chains of buckets, to saw wood, to press oil from seeds, and even to make paper. In France, Joseph and Etienne Montgolfier, sons of an Annonay papermaker whose factory was in a windmill, harnessed the energy of burning straw to inflate hot air balloons, and opened the way to conquest of the sky.

The Steam Age came about through an early 18th-century energy crisis, when English iron manufacturers ran out of charcoal for their furnaces — they had chopped down all the forests in the Sussex countryside. Switching to pit coal, they found their mines quickly flooded, and a way was sought to pump them dry. Thomas Savery, an ingenious mechanic, invented a device in which hot steam condensed suddenly in an iron chamber, creating a vacuum that sucked the water up from the mine shafts. The Savery

A German engineer in 1933 designed this amazing 1,000-foot-tall wind generator, which was never built. The only wind generator built for an American electric utility produced 1,250 kilowatts in Vermont before one of its blades failed in 1947.

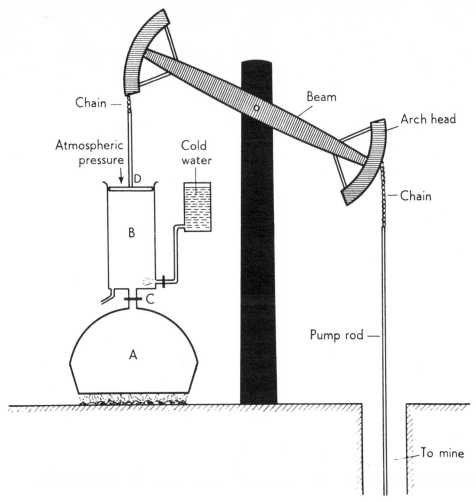

Thomas Newcomen invented the first crude steam engine with a piston, driven upward by steam and sucked down by cooling the cylinder with water.

machine was improved by Thomas Newcomen, whose machine was the first crude steam engine with a piston, driven upward by a blast of steam, and sucked down again by rapidly cooling the cylinder with cold water.

A Scottish engineer, James Watt, further improved on Newcomen's engine after studying a model in Glasgow University — he used a separate condenser to cool the steam; converted the piston stroke to rotary motion with a sun-and-planet gear; and added a centrifugal governor, one of the first uses of *feedback,* an essential element of modern automation.

Steam engines soon were powering England's textile mills, steamboats, even experimental aircraft. In 1830 the steam locomotive Rocket opened the age of railroading, which in nineteenth-century America brought about a national unification that forms a major part of our romantic folklore of the Old West.

The first transatlantic steam vessel, the British *Clermont,* in 1807 doomed the era of wind-powered clipper ships, its two paddlewheels working like

*Nineteenth-century America was unified with steels rails to support steam-driven loco-
motives that burned wood and coal for fuel.*

undershot waterwheels in reverse. Just one century later the *Lusitania* and
the *Mauritania* introduced steam turbine engines to the blue-ribbon Atlantic
run. The biggest steamers of all — the *Queen Mary* and *Queen Elizabeth*,
launched in the 1930's—finally retired when overseas air travel made
them obsolete.

Steam engines convert heat into mechanical and/or electrical energy
with an efficiency of only about 30 percent. A somewhat better energy
converter is the internal combustion engine, whose efficiency is roughly
only 50 percent.

Heedless of this energy waste, the world today has become dependent
on the automobile, which has radically changed our way of life. People
no longer stay home for recreation — the term is now synonymous with
travel, getting away for the weekend or on longer vacations, often towing
homes behind them.

The Automobile Age, of course, runs on fossil fuel, primarily gasoline

History's first oil well was drilled near Titusville, Pa., on August 27, 1859, by Edwin L. Drake (in top hat).

and diesel oil, yet when the first oil well was drilled in America, at Titusville, Pennsylvania, in 1859, the major demand was for "coal oil" (kerosene), to light the lamps of the world at a time when whales were being slaughtered in record numbers for whale oil. Within a week after Edwin Laurentine Drake struck oil in Titusville, the place was swarming with "wildcatters." By 1862, more than 1,500,000 gallons of kerosene and other petroleum products passed through the Port of New York.

Rich new oil fields were struck in Texas, Oklahoma, Louisiana, and other states, and by the time Detroit geared to mass automobile production in 1915, the oil industry and the auto industry were irrevocably wedded. The process of thermal cracking made oil refining profitable — the refiner not only could separate his raw material, he could transform it.

World War II spurred further development of refinery techniques with its heavy demand for high-octane aviation fuel, and since then a whole new economy has sprung up around petroleum — the massive petro-

The Steam Age changed the world's life style by introducing such wonders as the steam hammer, a steam flying machine, steam-powered ocean liners, and horseless steam carriages.

chemical industry. Today we produce some 50 billion pounds of organic chemicals in some 3,000 varieties, to make everything from tires to synthetic silk stockings.

The corner gas station remains the biggest outlet for gasoline. Since the first one was opened in 1907, the demand has finally outstripped the supply. In 1970 production soared past *two billion* 42-gallon barrels, still not enough.

Coal mining now runs to more than 600,000,000 tons a year, with more than half going to electric utility companies for steam generation. As the most abundant of all fossil fuels, the world supply of coal may last two hundred years or so, at our present rate of consumption, but the price in ravaged land will be high. Under a five-year, 10-billion-dollar energy development program, drafted for the government at Cornell University in 1973, a plan to strip-mine *one billion tons* of coal a year from surface mines by 1985 is projected, plus another 800,000,000 tons from underground mines to meet short-term energy needs.

Many inventions have been born of battle, including a way to make "artificial" gas, initially to fill Civil War reconnaissance balloons in the field. Here Professor T. S. C. Lowe inflates his Intrepid *with hydrogen, produced by pouring sulphuric acid over old horseshoes and nails in field wagon vats.*

As an energy source of giant magnitude, natural gas was largely ignored until the 1920's. A combination of two things made it profitable—discovery of large pools of natural gas in the midcontinent and southwest regions of the United States, and development of welded seamless steel pipes to deliver it to major cities.

Prior to this time, manufactured gas was popular, made by injecting steam over hot coke. The product, called water-gas, was perfected by a Civil War balloonist, Professor T.S.C. Lowe, who had earlier developed a way to make hydrogen in the field, to inflate his reconnaissance balloons. Natural gas has, in a half century, surpassed electricity in both industrial and home use, in heating, refrigeration, and air conditioning.

By 1950, natural gas production, distribution, and consumption had reached 8,500,000,000,000,000 British thermal units, more than five-and-one-half times the total electrical energy generated in all public and private powerplants.

Today, however, both gas and electric companies, which had struggled

"OTTO"
GAS AND GASOLINE
ENGINES,
1-3 to 100 horse power
Can be used in cities
or in country inde-
pendent of gas works
or gas machines.
No Boiler.
No Danger.
No Engineer.

OVER
33,000 SOLD.
OTTO GAS ENGINE WORKS, PHILADELPHIA.

Induction	Compression	Power	Exhaust
Inlet valve opens. Piston moves down and draws fuel into cylinder.	Both valves closed. Piston moves up and compresses mixture.	Spark at plug ignites mixture, forcing down piston and driving crankshaft.	Exhaust valve o Piston rises a expels waste pro of combustie

Some people blame the 1974 energy crisis on invention of the internal combustion engine, perfected in 1867 in Deutz, Germany, by Nikolaus Otto, whose name is given to its operating principle, the Otto Cycle. Faced with a shortage of fossil fuels, today's inventors are tackling the problem of developing practical steam automobiles (lower left) and hydrogen-powered cars (lower right). Main obstacle to mass use of hydrogen car is storage—how to compress enough hydrogen into a fuel tank to provide a driving range of about 200 miles, between refills or recharges.

to capture the home market, have switched to a new form of salesman-ship. "What we have now," says a spokesman for the electric industry, "is the death of a salesman. We're trying to get people to use less energy, not more!"

Cutaway view of pressurized water nuclear reactor (note size of man at right).

OTHER ENERGY SOURCES

CLOSING THE "energy gap" is something that won't come about overnight. In 1973 President Richard M. Nixon proposed a major effort called Project Independence 1980 which, ironically, threatened to overshadow the two-hundredth anniversary of American Independence in 1976. Yet to meet our total energy needs by 1980 would be a staggering feat — in the next decade, says the Congressional Joint Committee on Atomic Energy, the United States will consume as much oil and gas as it has in its past history.

"We have used the cream of our oil, gas, and coal resources," said the Committee. The answer, they underscored, lay in an accelerated shift to other energy sources, mainly nuclear.

On January 1, 1974, the world had barely moved into the Atomic Age of nuclear power; a total of 167 nuclear reactors in 17 countries were producing only 60,000 megawatts (a megawatt is 1,000,000 watts), roughly 4.5 percent of the total world electric generating capacity. By 1980, deadline

Jackpile Mine, New Mexico, is largest open-pit uranium mine in United States.

for Project Independence's goal of energy self-sufficiency, an estimated 350 nuclear power plants will meet only 14 percent of the world's energy needs.

Faced with the prospect of ravaging our limited supply of fossil fuels, to keep pace with energy demands as a stop-gap, until nuclear power becomes widely available we have a number of other energy sources to turn to — but again, time is short.

Strip-mining the surface of the Earth for coal, which accounts for 44 percent of our coal production, is a dramatic illustration of land abuse, in the words of Supreme Court Justice William O. Douglas. Compounds of sulfur associated with coal produce sulfuric acid when exposed to air, causing widespread damage to plant life. As another example of land abuse, the Kennecott Copper mine at Brigham Canyon, Utah, the world's largest open pit mine, engulfed an entire town of 10,000 population, leaving only scarred earth.

Oil companies in 1974 bid more than 200 million dollars on leases to strip-mine some 5,000 acres of oil-shale-bearing land in Colorado, a tiny corner of the Green River Formation covering 16,500 square miles of Colorado, Utah, and Wyoming. Here lie an estimated 3 trillion barrels of a substance called *kerogen,* held in rocks called *marl.* Heated to 900 degrees, the kerogen cooks out into shale oil, which can be refined into gasoline and other petroleum products. In addition to oil shale, another source of fossil fuels largely neglected are deposits of tar sands, the world's largest being the Athabasca Field in northern Alberta, Canada, with reserves totaling some 300 billion barrels.

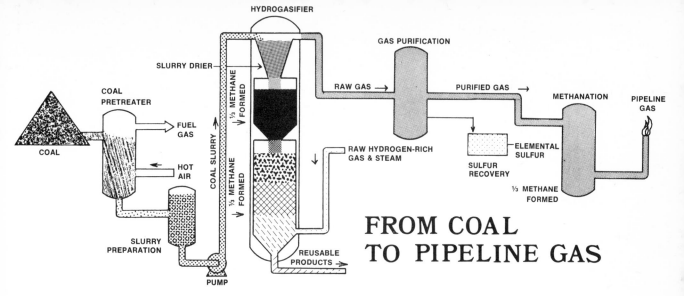

FROM COAL TO PIPELINE GAS

Hydrogasification of coal by HYGAS Process starts by mixing pulverized coal with light oil to form a muddy slurry. In the hydrogasifier, rising gas of methane, carbon oxides, hydrogen, and steam is heated by a bed of hot coals, reacts with the coal slurry to form two-thirds of the end product—methane. The gas is then scrubbed clean and further refined in methanation section.

Four other non-fossil, non-atomic energy sources remain in our budget of potential power — direct and indirect solar energy, tidal energy, and geothermal energy.

On a small scale, direct use of solar energy has been around a long time. Curved mirrors were used to collect the sun's rays and focus them on water stills in ancient times. Thousands of solar water heaters are in use today in modern homes. Some years ago, the author hooked up a swimming pool filter system to a coil of black plastic pipe on the roof of a cabana, saved fuel bills by using direct solar energy to heat the pool.

In 1973 Congress took official notice of solar energy, when Representative Mike McCormack (D-Wash.) sponsored legislation to authorize a 50-million-dollar five-year program of intense research, aimed at tapping this source in several possible ways. One was to utilize massive banks of solar cells on a satellite in synchronous orbit, 22,300 mile out in space, to convert sunlight to electricity and beam it to Earth.

Spacecraft have utilized solar energy for several years to produce electricity with panels covered with what are called photovoltaic cells. These were developed in 1954 by the Bell Telephone Laboratories, initially for use aboard communications satellites. Such cells consist of thin wafers of ultrapure silicon, to which traces of arsenic and boron are added. In bright sunlight, these cells convert radiant solar energy into electricity with an efficiency as high as 16 percent.

One exciting proposal in turning to a "sunshine economy" for power is a large scale, floating, ocean-borne generating station, in which sunlight would be concentrated to convert sea water into liquid hydrogen and

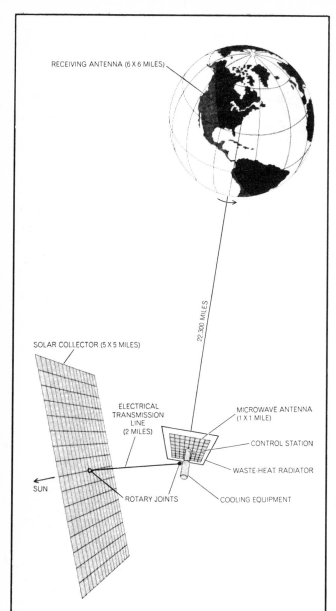

RECEIVING ANTENNA (6 X 6 MILES)

22,300 MILES

SOLAR COLLECTOR (5 X 5 MILES)

ELECTRICAL
TRANSMISSION
LINE
(2 MILES)

MICROWAVE ANTENNA
(1 X 1 MILE)

CONTROL STATION

WASTE-HEAT RADIATOR

SUN

ROTARY JOINTS

COOLING EQUIPMENT

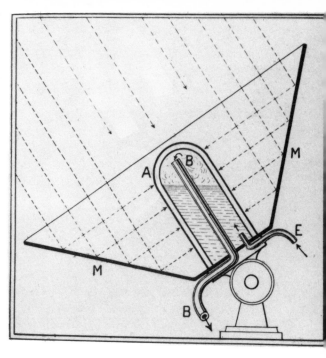

*Similar to 18th-century solar oven (above), modern scheme
for direct use of solar energy are under study. One Congres
sional committee proposes to launch into a 22,300-mil
synchronous orbit a solar panel of 25 square miles, to gather
energy from Sun, convert it into electricity, and beam it to
a 36-square-mile microwave antenna on Earth. A test facility
at Langley Research Center will use solar energy to heat and
cool buildings.*

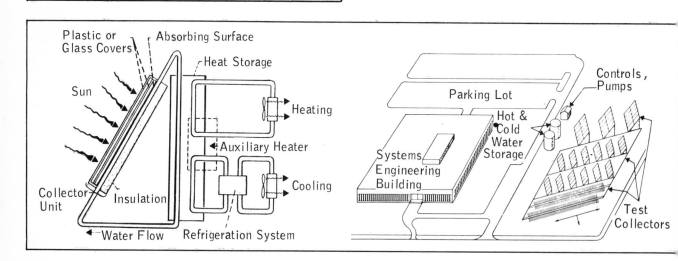

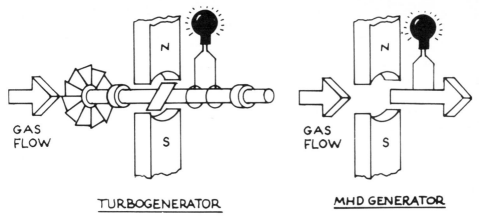

TURBOGENERATOR   MHD GENERATOR

Large-scale power plants may someday convert high-temperature gas streams directly into electrical energy by magnetohydrodynamic (MHD) process, using principle that ionized gas is electrically conductive. Current results from blowing gas across a magnetic field (see p. 75).

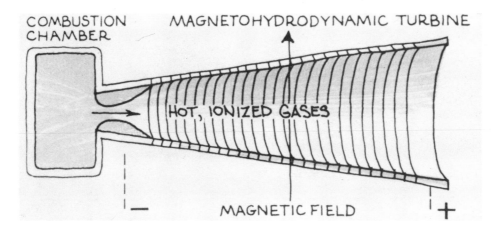

COMBUSTION CHAMBER   MAGNETOHYDRODYNAMIC TURBINE

HOT, IONIZED GASES

MAGNETIC FIELD

oxygen, easily transported in large cryogenic (super-cool) tanks or through pipes, for later conversion to electric power by combustion.

Ocean thermal plants are still another possibility; scientists say there is enough heat in the Gulf Stream alone to meet the United States' power needs 200 times over. In such a conversion system, heat from the ocean's surface causes propanes in a boiler to evaporate into a high-pressure vapor, which drives a turbine to generate electricity. Cold water, drawn from the ocean depths, in turn cools the propane vapor back into liquid form for recycling.

Two scientists at the University of Houston proposed a futuristic solar energy system in which mirrors, spread over a square mile of ground, would focus the Sun's rays on a solar furnace and boiler atop a 1,500-foot tower at the center. Heat from the boiler, at a temperature of 2,000 degrees, would be converted into electric power in a process called magnetohydrodynamic (MHD) conversion.

In 1936 Hoover Dam on Colorado River began producing electricity at 1,345 megawatts capacity.

At Mont-Louis in the French Pyrenees, an experimental solar furnace uses 3,500 small mirrors to concentrate sunlight on a single crucible, producing temperatures of 5,400°F. for high-heat research work.

We come now to indirect uses of solar energy, which include harnessing the wind, largely impractical on a large scale, and harnessing the power in the flow of streams. The world's total water-power capacity amounts to some 3 trillion watts, while less than 10 percent is at present utilized in hydroelectric conversion systems.

In 1920, when transmission of electricity over long distances became possible, a Federal Power Commission was created by Congress to develop hydroelectric power sites on navigable waters and public lands. The first large FPC hydroelectric project got under way in 1928, with passage of the Boulder Canyon Act, authorizing construction of 726-foot-high Hoover Dam on the Colorado River. This project had multiple purposes — navigation, flood control, irrigation, municipal water supply to major

Portal Powerhouse in Sierra Nevada is one of eight powerhouses in Big Creek hydroelectric system, "the world's hardest working water."

cities in Southern California, and creation of a power development with a capacity of more than 1,300,000 kilowatts.

In the Pacific Northwest Bonneville Dam, with 518,400 kilowatts capacity, was built by the U.S. Army Corps of Engineers at the head of tidewater on the Columbia River, while on the upper Columbia the Grand Coulee Dam, with nearly 2,000,000 kilowatts capacity, was built by the Bureau of Reclamation, backing up water to the Canadian boundary.

In 1916 Muscle Shoals in northwestern Alabama was selected as a hydroelectric dam site, to supply power for the synthetic production of nitrates for munitions and fertilizers.

The nation's first large-scale, multi-purpose hydroelectric development was constructed at the turn of the century by the Southern California Edison Company in the High Sierras. Its six manmade lakes and eight powerhouses can supply electricity to a city of 1,000,000 people, yet today over 90 percent of SCE's generating capacity is produced by steam plants.

France's Rance River tidal power facility draws energy from 44-foot tides that flow into estuary from English Channel, then return through turbine traps that produce 10 megawatts of power per turbine.

The mountain lakes not only supply hydroelectric power, they are used for flood control, irrigation, and recreation.

Wind power, one of the earliest sources of energy, is harnessed today by modern windmills that run farm generators, but the unpredictability of the winds makes them relatively useless as large-scale power sources. However, in the Midwest, where winds average 12 miles an hour or more, studies show that wind-driven generators can practically decompose water into hydrogen and oxygen for storage under pressure, to be recombined in fuel cells for pollution-free generation of steady electricity.

Turning to tidal power as an energy source, the world's potential is believed to approximate 64 billion watts, or 2 percent of the world's potential water power. Though only a fractional answer to the energy crisis, tidal power is now in use, as in an ambitious project recently completed in France, harnessing the power of tides in the English Channel with a dam across the Rance River.

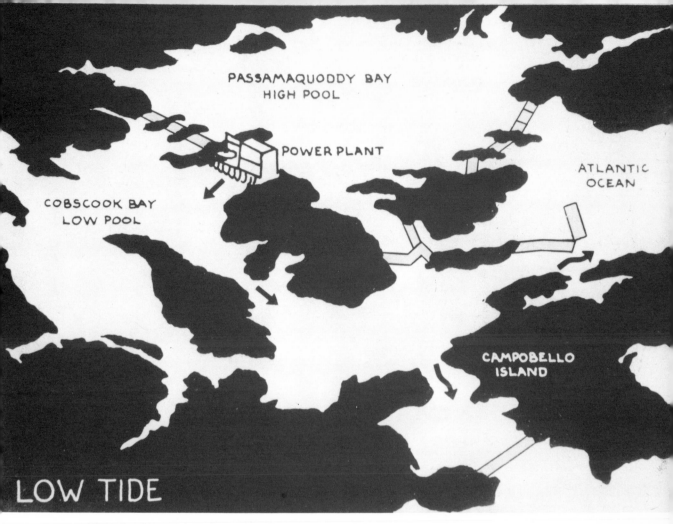

PASSAMAQUODDY BAY
HIGH POOL

POWER PLANT

ATLANTIC
OCEAN

COBSCOOK BAY
LOW POOL

CAMPOBELLO
ISLAND

LOW TIDE

A favorite dream of engineers is to harness the surging spring tides in Passamaquoddy Bay, an arm of the Bay of Fundy between Maine and New Brunswick, where more than 700,000 horsepower in two billion tons of trapped water could produce 40 million kilowatts of electrical energy.

Since 1966 the Rance River has been producing electric power with 24 turbogenerator units, energized by tidal water flowing out of a nine-square-mile tidal pool behind the dam. Tidal ranges of as much as 44 feet fill the Rance estuary, then rush out through funnel-shaped tubes, spinning giant turbine blades shaped like ships screws. Each turbine produces 10 megawatts of electrical energy.

Tidal power first caught the imagination of the late President Franklin D. Roosevelt, who as early as 1920 was impressed with the awesome rush of tides in Passamaquoddy Bay between Maine and Canada. Here the average spring tidal range exceeds 23 feet; each 12 hours more than two billion tons of water surge in and out of the Bay. Harnessing an estimated 700,000 horsepower, enough to produce as much as 40 million kilowatts of electrical power, remains the goal of the Passamaquoddy Tidal Power Project.

One of the greatest breakthroughs in developing new energy sources

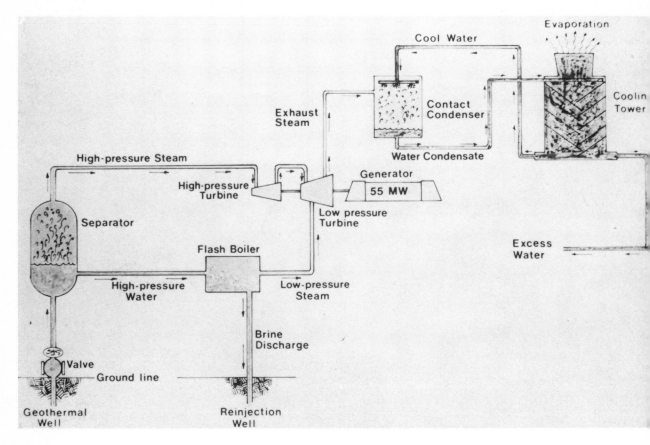

Geothermal steam plants, now in operation in many countries, tap the virtually limitless source of energy from radioactivity within the Earth's core. Geothermal steam is separated from water for reinjecting. The steam, under high pressure, drives turbines to run generators. Today orbiting Earth Resources Technology Satellites are on the lookout for hidden geothermal fields.

may well be in the area of geothermal (Earth heat) power, locked in the very heart of our planet. Natural radioactivity, present in small amounts in all rocks but in large amounts at the Earth's molten center, continues to heat the core. This heat flows outward in small amounts, producing occasional hot springs and volcanic activity.

In some areas, faults in the Earth's mantle, which encases its core, allow molten rock, called *magma,* to flow quite near the surface. Surface water may come into contact with hot magma, and rise to the surface as hot water or steam. Old Faithful, the famous geyser at Yellowstone National Park, is a good example.

The world's first geothermal power plant, constructed near Lardarello, Italy, in 1904, still produces 365,000 kilowatts of electric power from a dry-steam geothermal reservoir. Smaller geothermal plants are operating in New Zealand, Iceland, Japan, and Russia. The potential for geothermal energy use in the United States is roughly 6,000,000 kilowatts, by the year 2,000.

The Geysers geothermal steam field in California's Sonoma County, producing 400,000 kilowatts of electric power, is world's largest such plant. Units on skyline went into operation in 1972.

For some time there was legal confusion over whether or not natural steam was a mineral. In 1970 Congress passed clarifying legislation, authorizing the Department of the Interior to encourage development of geothermal resources on public land.

As early as 1847 geothermal energy was known to exist in California, when a bear hunter discovered a canyon with steam pouring out of the ground along its length. Called The Geysers, it became a tourist attraction, but not until the 1950's was the area, on private property, leased for power production. Here, in the rugged Mayacmas Mountains north of San Francisco, is the world's largest geothermal power plant, with ten units producing nearly 400,000 kilowatts of power. It is the only producing geothermal plant in the United States.

Under an Atomic Energy Commission grant, the University of California is now energetically developing other sites. One region of great promise lies in what is called the Salton Sink in Southern California, stretching from the Salton Sea across the Mexican border to the Sea of

Cerro Prieto geothermal steam plant in Baja California.

Cortez (Gulf of California). Some 30 miles south of the border lies an extinct volcano called *Cerro Prieto* (the Black Hill). Here, some years ago, the Mexican Government solved one of its own energy crises by building a successful geothermal steam plant. It now lights border towns from Mexicali and Calexico to Tijuana, and has given the area a huge economic boost by supplying power for small manufacturing plants.

Cerro Prieto is a good case history of what can be done by men with imagination and drive. The story goes back to 1939, when Mexico's President Lazaro Cardenas expropriated foreign-owned petroleum properties and formed the Federal Electricity Commission, to help raise his country's peasants from poverty. One organizer of the Commission was Luis F. de Anda, an engineer whose family had made a fortune turning hot springs into health spas.

De Anda saw a great power potential in the Cerro Prieto hot springs.

Volcanic heat at Cerro Prieto produces 75,000 kilowatts of power.

He brought in experts from Iceland, where geothermal steam had been harnessed since 1925. In 1961 drillers struck boiling water 2,000 feet under the Cerro Prieto volcanic field. Japanese bankers financed a 16-million-dollar facility, now able to produce 75 megawatts of energy from "flashed" steam — a process that separates boiling water and wet steam, releasing the latter to turn turbo-generators.

Today, orbiting Earth Resources Technology Satellites search continuously for new geothermal fields. By 1974 geothermal leases of public lands had already run into millions of dollars. Dr. Robert W. Rex, president of Republic Geothermal, Inc., a former director of the Institute of Geophysics and Planetary Physics at the University of California Riverside, sees a potential to supply the nation's entire energy needs from what is called the hot-rock geothermal method.

By this process, surface water would be pumped down through deep

wells to a depth of nearly three miles, into hot magma. The rock immediately above would be fractured by atomic explosions, allowing the heated water to flow back to the surface through a second well.

With the virtually limitless quantity of stored heat inside the Earth harnessed, our energy problem might indeed be solved. Basically, we would be utilizing radioactivity in the Earth's core, a variation of two other atomic energy sources described in the concluding chapters — those of nuclear fission, already in use, and of nuclear fusion, which many scientists believe will be our ultimate power supply.

COSMIC ENERGY—
CAN WE TAP THE SOURCE?

Visible plasma in Monoceros Nebula reveals cosmic energy.

TO UNDERSTAND the great balance of energy in the universe has been a challenge to the human intellect since the first creative caveman sat before his fire, made by rubbing two sticks together, and gazed at constellations of stars wheeling overhead. The heat from his tiny fire, the wind blowing through the trees, the crash of a distant surf, all shared something in common with the orderly movement of the heavens — energy in motion.

All energy on Earth, with the exception of nuclear energy within matter itself, springs from the star we call our Sun; without sunlight there could be no photosynthesis to make the large molecular structures of food we call carbohydrates. The Sun's gravitational pull creates the tides, its radiant energy heats the top of the atmosphere, where much of the world's weather is now known to be born.

The whole cosmos seethes with energy in various forms — gravity, heat, light, nuclear activity. By far the greatest is gravitational energy, little understood until Dr. Albert Einstein in 1905 concluded it was some-

Orbiting Astronomical Observatory Copernicus, launched in 1973, uses solar panels to power six on-board telescopes searching for ultra-violet and X-ray stellar energy sources. Copernicus reports on what it sees by a system called telemetry.

thing all mass shares, something that can be changed into energy in the form of heat or light.

Through this process — changing gravity into heat or light — the whole universe, cosmologists think, is slowly dying, a disorder called *entropy*. A near example is our own Sun, a gigantic nuclear fusion reactor that consumes hydrogen atoms at a rate of 657 million tons a second, converting them into 653 million tons of helium. The lost 4 million tons have been transformed into radiant energy.

Solar energy reaches Earth in the form of a *plasma*. Plasma is often called the fourth state of matter; matter may exist as solid, liquid, gas, or plasma. When a gas is superheated it becomes a plasma — the electrons and nuclei of atoms break free of each other. Free nuclei are called ions, and the breakup process is called ionization.

The study of particle behavior in a plasma is called magnetohydrodynamics (MHD), and already man has learned how to apply its prin-

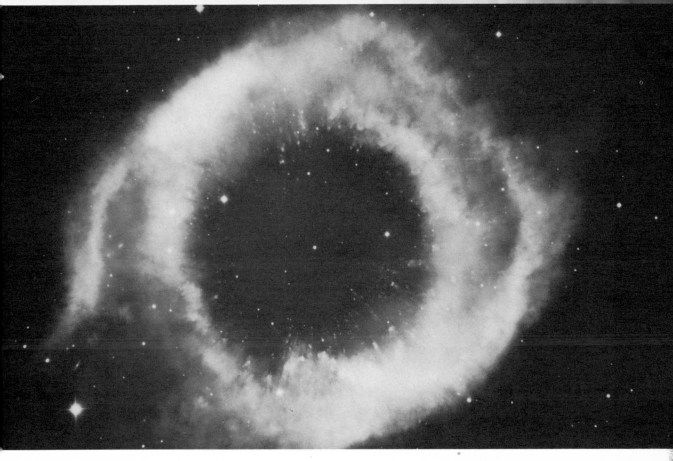

One of the least understood energy sources in the cosmos is that responsible for rare planetary nebulae, such as this beautiful, doughnut-shaped one in the constellation Aquarius, designated NGC 7293 by astronomers. The gaseous ring, made up largely of hydrogen plasma, glows with eerie luminiscence produced by strong ultraviolet radiation from super-hot stars inside the ring. The study of such ionized plasmas in space may help us to design future nuclear energy devices on Earth.

ciples, in devices that extract electrical energy from ionized gas at high temperatures. Before he could achieve this, he had to study plasmas in space, the only laboratory where unconfined plasmas can be observed at very low temperatures and densities.

For years scientists believed that particle energy in plasmas from the Sun occurred only briefly, following eruptions called solar flares. Exploration of space by robot satellites has shown that a continuous flux of plasma comes from the Sun, because of its high surface temperatures. This solar plasma is called the solar wind.

Satellite investigation further showed that the solar wind pulls the Sun's magnetic field out in curving arms like giant cork screws, called Archimedean spirals. It's like what you would see from an apartment house balcony, if you looked down on a rotary garden sprinkler, and is sometimes called the *garden hose effect* for this reason.

Scientists now hope to duplicate on Earth the Sun's fantastic production

SIZE OF EARTH

Huge solar eruption photographed during Skylab 3 mission, in a remarkable picture that reveals for the first time that helium erupting from the Sun can hold together at altitudes of up to 500,000 miles.

of energy, by fusing hydrogen atoms into helium atoms on a smaller scale, and extracting electrical energy from ionized plasmas, contained in magnetic fields shaped like the Sun's Archimedean spirals. We have a limitless supply of fuel—the hydrogen isotope deuterium—in the seas.

Before man could attain energy conversion from hydrogen fusion he had to duplicate here on Earth the tremendous amount of heat inside the Sun — on the order of 100,000,000° Centigrade. In the last chapter the story is told how man attained a fusion reaction, in the hydrogen bomb of 1951, and now has found a way to achieve virtually limitless energy through *controlled* thermonuclear fusion.

Although a practical nuclear *fusion* plant is still years away, we have in the meantime tapped another nuclear source of energy, through atomic *fission* (splitting) of such heavy elements as uranium and plutonium. We already have put it to work in a growing number of reactors, in which heat released by fission is converted into electricity.

Astronomers believe bright arms in spiral galaxies consist of newly-formed stars left behind by passage of rotating hydrodynamic-gravitational wave in the galactic disc. Without this spinning energy, galaxy would collapse through gravitational contraction, and the Earth would never have been born.

Understanding the nature of the atom, and finally splitting it for the production of energy, came about through the study of similar processes in the cosmos. The atom essentially is a tiny solar system, with different numbers of electrons orbiting a Sun-like nucleus.

In seeking an answer to the relationship between mass and energy, man looked far beyond his own solar system, to the edge of the Universe. What he found was exciting and disturbing — many bright stars shine brilliantly for a few million years, then die in a blaze of fire as supernovae. Why?

One explanation is that some elemental shock wave of gravity is involved. A galaxy (cluster of stars) may lie dormant for 100,000,000 years, its interstellar gas field then suddenly compressing with a burst of energy to form new stars. Such newly formed star clusters become visible as luminous spiral arms sweeping around and around a nebula. Is it possible, astronomers wonder, that a cyclic rhythm exists, energizing

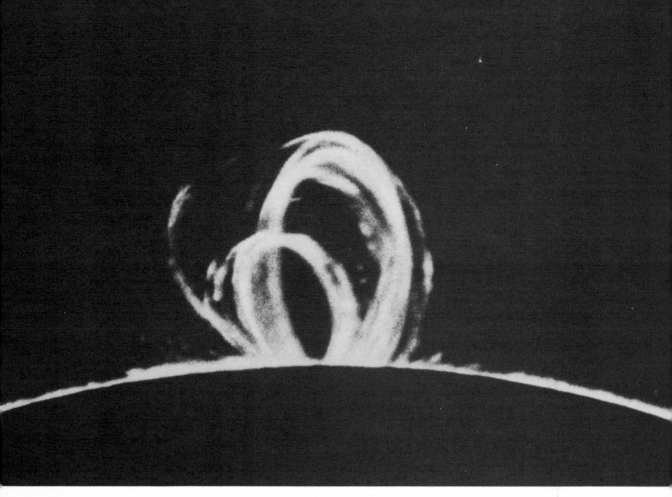

Largest eruptive-type solar prominence ever seen was photographed June 4, 1946, at the High Altitude Observatory, Boulder, Colo. Within a single hour it grew as large as the Sun itself, then died out. Flare was largely hydrogen.

creation of new stars as these spiral nebulae whirl through space? Is this the way our own solar system came into existence?

There are still greater cosmic energy sources, such as the radio galaxies and quasars (quasi-stellar radio sources) at the fringes of space, producing energies millions of times greater than the most brilliant supernova. Of these we know virtually nothing, only that they exist. Perhaps a future Einstein will explain them in a new formula as beautiful as $E=mc^2$ — who knows?

Tapping cosmic sources of energy may become possible at some distant date; already research is going on, on Earth and aboard orbiting spacecraft, to understand better the nature of mysterious particles of radiation called *cosmic rays.*

Whether or not we'll ever find a way to harness the power of cosmic rays, we know it exists, and we can measure it. Its distinctive feature is a unique concentration of energy in single elementary particles. Like solar

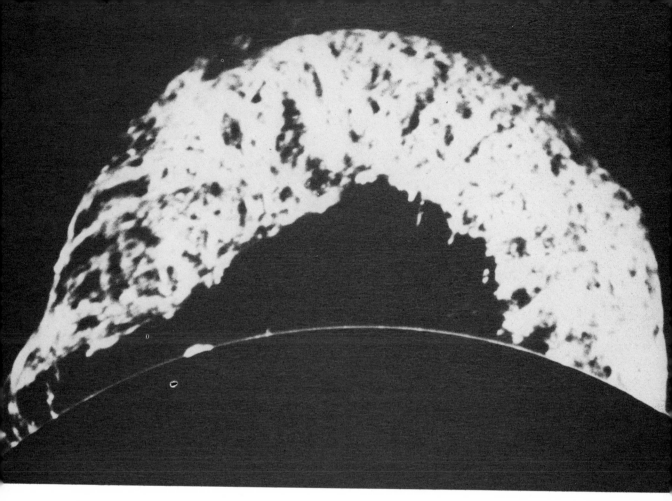

Looping outward from the Sun, hydrogen solar flare at left has twisted into writhing, doughnut-shaped coil of energy, its heated plasma contained by magnetic lines of force. Such magnetic containment is part of modern fusion reactor design.

winds that produce brilliant displays of aurora borealis, they consist mainly of protons, the nuclei of hydrogen atoms.

The total energy from all cosmic rays entering our atmosphere in any given time is no greater than starlight, and 100,000,000 times less than the radiant energy from the Sun, yet these rays provide us with a valuable source of scientific information. From studying their effects we understand better the interchange of energy between matter and radiation and electromagnetic theory, in itself vitally important in the design of fusion reactors.

Perhaps more important, these made possible the discovery of most of the known elementary particles of matter, which so far as we know are the basis of all energy. This was achieved by using cosmic rays as a super-microscope, in a sense, able to peer into the heart of an atom. This came about from the discovery that, when a cosmic ray strikes the nucleus of an atom, it interacts with the smallest part of which the nucleus is composed.

Beautiful Horsehead Nebula in Orion, photographed in red light, shows prominently a dark cloud of matter extending upward and blocking out starlight behind it. Such clouds may be hydrogen plasma, part of the cosmos's limitless energy source.

Here was a tool to dig into the very source of all energy, through better knowledge of what are called Fundamental Particles, the basic constituents of matter and energy. Earlier, atoms had been considered to be the smallest possible particles, until, through cosmic ray studies, man had penetrated the heart of the atom and looked into the future.

For the first time the true nature of energy, and its relation to matter, was understood. By the mid-1920's, the concept of *quantum mechanics* was born of this research. Quantum mechanics, less publicized than relativity, provided rich new fields for investigation of energy phenomena so small-scaled they fail to fit classical descriptions.

The motions of electrons or nuclei inside atoms and molecules stood revealed, and the energies required to hold them all together were better understood. It was found that the number of electrons in a neutral atom is the same as what chemists call its atomic number — one for hydrogen, two for helium, and so on.

Spiral galaxy NGC 4594 in constellation Virgo, seen edge on, demonstrates cosmic energy struggle. Centrifugal force of its spinning arms prevents it from collapsing under gravitational energy, the predominant form of energy throughout the Universe.

Dynamics of the orbits of electrons also became better understood, and in these miniature solar systems man saw the ultimate energy source, duplicating energy processes of the cosmos which exist on a grander scale. At his death in 1955, Einstein was trying to get it all together with what he called the Unified Field Theory.

Of the 92 naturally occurring chemical elements, only a few behave in a manner defiant of the principles of conservation of matter, in being radioactive, and therefore are the key to huge sources of energy. Radioactive elements and their isotopes (other forms) are relatively heavy, with large atomic numbers and large numbers of electrons.

By splitting such an atom apart, scientists wondered, could not its energy be released? It was a dangerous question, one that would be answered under the pressure of World War II, with creation of the atomic bomb. With the A-bomb man proved he could split the atom; controlling its gigantic release of energy.

SPLITTING THE ATOM FOR POWER

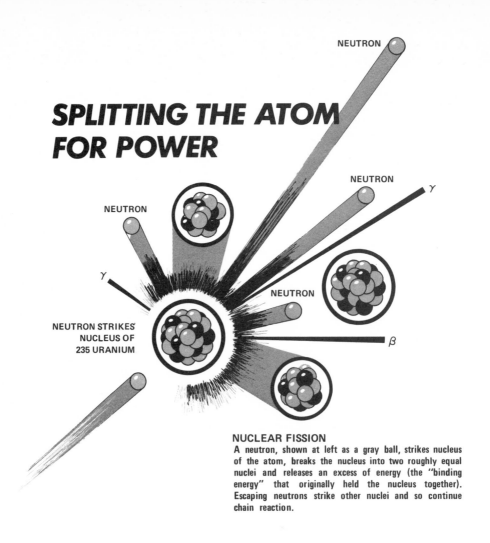

NUCLEAR FISSION
A neutron, shown at left as a gray ball, strikes nucleus of the atom, breaks the nucleus into two roughly equal nuclei and releases an excess of energy (the "binding energy" that originally held the nucleus together). Escaping neutrons strike other nuclei and so continue chain reaction.

IF QUANTUM mechanics disclosed the energies locked inside an atom, the question to be answered was, how can man release those energies and put them to practical use? Scientists knew they were working with something far more terrible than dynamite. If they started up a "chain reaction" —where one atom splits in two, then splits another atom, and so on— could it be controlled?

The story of how man learned to split the atom and release the energy stored inside is one of the great detective stories of all time. Like Sherlock Holmes, nuclear scientists, working without a single tangible clue, turned to sheer intellect to solve the problem. Dr. Albert Einstein, a theoretical physicist who hadn't been inside a laboratory for years, first conceived the brilliant notion that mass and energy were one and the same, and that somehow one could be transmuted into the other.

Einstein in 1905 put it all down in his classic equation: $E = mc^2$ — the total energy (E) locked in a mass (m) is equal to m multiplied by the square of the velocity of light (c). Doubters shook their heads; if Einstein were right, a single pound of any substance, converted into energy, would be equivalent to 10,000,000 tons of TNT! Here was a source of riches more valuable to man than all the gold in the world!

Through cosmic ray studies in 1932 Einstein's theory of relativity was proven in the laboratory, when tracks of cosmic rays were photographed in what is known as a cloud chamber. Cosmic ray particles zapping through a mist of water vapor leave tracks that can be photographed. The particles are called *photons.*

This development threw a whole new light on our understanding of radiant energy; it showed that light exists not only in the form of electromagnetic waves, but as fast-moving particles as well. Understanding this dual character of light, and of matter, was a break-through in quantum mechanics. Further studies of nuclear behavior, still using cosmic rays in cloud chambers as a sort of super microscope, led to surprising results. Then, in 1939, two German chemists accidentally discovered a way to unlock the energy inside an atom, while bombarding a chunk of uranium with a stream of neutrons to make a heavier element. Instead, they produced a tiny particle of barium, an element much lighter than uranium. They'd split an uranium nucleus into two lighter elements, whose total weight was less than the original. The balance had been converted into energy.

When World War II exploded, about this time, a massive effort was launched to find a way to make this energy-release reaction self-sustaining, in a chain reaction. This was achieved on December 2, 1942, when history's first atomic pile was ignited in a squash court of Stagg Field, at the University of Chicago. A group of scientists, led by Enrico Fermi, knew they had made history in achieving *controlled release of energy* from atoms.

The problem they solved was how to make sure enough freed neutrons from a split atom of uranium could be used to split other atoms. When one atom of uranium splits, it releases two or three neutrons, but these travel at such high speeds they're likely to miss their targets. To slow them down, Fermi encased the uranium fuel in a huge pile of graphite, which tended to retard their velocities.

To eliminate the possibility of a runaway nuclear reaction, a number of neutron-absorbing cadmium rods were inserted into the *pile,* as the core of the first reactor soon became known. The success of this experiment led to the Manhattan Project, the greatest technological effort ever undertaken by man. The result was the frightful atomic bomb.

Actually, there were two different kinds of atomic bombs — the first, exploded at Alamogordo and over Nagasaki, was made from plutonium; the Hiroshima bomb used Uranium 235. Both involved virtual instanta-

Nuclear weapon of the "Fat Man" type detonated over Nagasaki, Japan, in World War II, weighed five tons, had an energy yield equivalent to 20,000 tons of high explosive. Fat Man was fueled with the isotope plutonium-239, the first man-made element ever made in a quantity large enough to see.

neous release of their vast potential energy, and both led to design of controlled nuclear power plants, using similar reactive processes.

Much had to be learned in a short time about the nature of the atom, before it could be harnessed for war or for peace. First, it was found that nuclei of any substance always have the same number of positively-charged protons, but may have a different number of neutrally-charged particles called neutrons.

Neutrons cannot be deflected by electrical fields, hence their ability to collide with and split a nucleus into two or more separate nuclei, accompanied by the release of large amounts of energy. Some elements are *fissionable* (can be split), others are not. Depending on the number of neutrons in the heart of an atom, it may take any of several different forms, called *isotopes.* The most common uranium isotopes are U-238 and U-235. The latter is fissionable, but the former is not, yet it is far more abundant, accounting for 99.3 percent of uranium in which both isotopes exist.

AEC's Oak Ridge, Tenn., Gaseous Diffusion Plant, built as a top-secret project during World War II to separate U-235 and U-238 isotopes, is one of three in United States producing enriched uranium for fuel elements in nuclear power plants. Others are at Paducah, Kentucky, and Portsmouth, Ohio.

The problem faced by the Manhattan Project, then, was to separate the two isotopes. This was accomplished in what is called a gaseous-diffusion plant, a $500,000,000 installation at Oak Ridge, Tennessee, half a mile in length. Inside the plant, uranium was combined with fluorine, to form a gaseous compound whose molecules could be separated.

It worked this way: gaseous uranium hexafluoride was pumped against a superfine screen, and the lighter U-235 particles penetrated it faster than the heavier U-238. The process was repeated thousands of times, before the concentration of the desired U-235 could be enriched from 0.7 percent of the mixture to an amazing 95 percent.

In another plant at Oak Ridge, by passing uranium tetrachloride gas, in an electrically charged state, through a strong magnetic field, the paths of the two isotopes, U-235 and U-238, were curved differently, a separation process that produced a U-235 concentrate 85 percent pure.

The plutonium bomb resulted from an entirely different project established by the government at Hanford, Washington, where a number

Four-unit, 2,000,000 kilowatt Pickering Generating Station of Ontario Hydro, on Lake Ontario, is the world's largest operating nuclear power station, designed by Atomic Energy of Canada Ltd.

of huge atomic piles were fueled with the more abundant and heavier uranium isotope U-238. These piles were allowed to simmer slowly, cooled by Columbia River water, while a strange transmutation took place, the first manmade change of one element to another, fulfilling the old alchemists' dream. Under neutron bombardment, the U-238 in raw uranium stock was slowly converted into isotope *Plutonium-239.*

Plutonium-239 is called a *fissile* isotope, one which can be split when bombarded with *slow* neutrons. In atomic fission, more than 99 percent of the neutrons produced are called *prompt* or *fast* neutrons, which are produced almost instantaneously. In some reactors, as many as *ten million generations* of prompt neutrons can be produced in a single second. It is easy to see that even a slight excess of neutrons could cause the intensity of a chain reaction to rapidly speed up.

Fortunately, some neutrons are released more slowly, through the decay of fission products rather than directly by fission. *Delayed* neutrons from

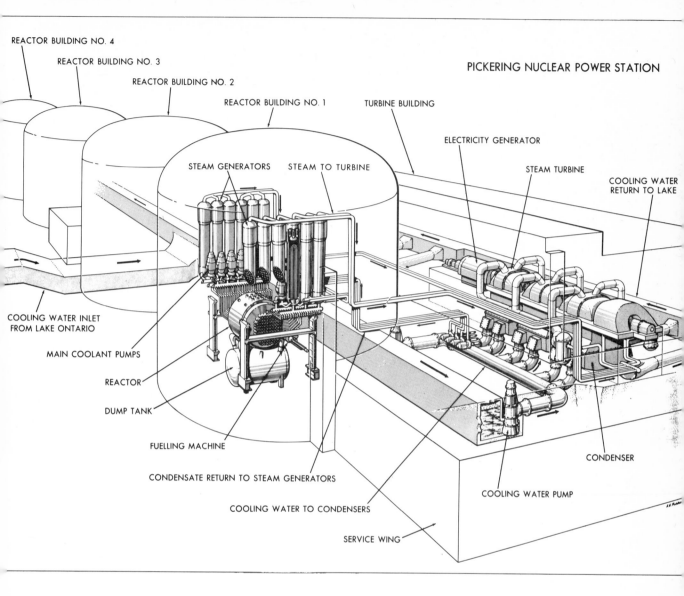

REACTOR BUILDING NO. 4

REACTOR BUILDING NO. 3

REACTOR BUILDING NO. 2

REACTOR BUILDING NO. 1

TURBINE BUILDING

ELECTRICITY GENERATOR

STEAM GENERATORS

STEAM TO TURBINE

STEAM TURBINE

COOLING WATER RETURN TO LAKE

COOLING WATER INLET FROM LAKE ONTARIO

MAIN COOLANT PUMPS

REACTOR

DUMP TANK

FUELLING MACHINE

CONDENSATE RETURN TO STEAM GENERATORS

COOLING WATER TO CONDENSERS

SERVICE WING

CONDENSER

COOLING WATER PUMP

fissioning U-235 have a "half-life" of about 13 seconds — the time it takes for half the atoms of the radioactive material to disintegrate. This gives time for safe control of the process.

In modern nuclear reactors, materials called *poisons* are used further to regulate the chain reactions. These poison elements include boron, cadmium, hafnium, and gadolinium, and are inserted inside the atomic piles in the form of "control rods" which can be withdrawn to start up the reactor, or reinserted to shut it down.

Depending on the velocity that the neutrons in a reactor travel, they are classed as either fast or slow (*thermal*) reactors. A neutron produced by fission has an energy of about 2,000,000 electron volts (2MeV), and if it is not absorbed by another nucleus, it bounces off other particles and finally reaches equilibrium. In this "thermal" state it possesses only 1/80,000,000th of its original energy.

Modern commercial water reactors are thermal reactors, because thermal

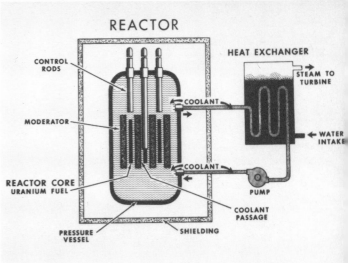

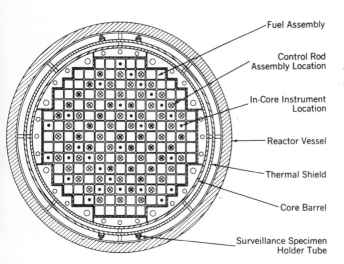

Fuel Assembly

Control Rod
Assembly Location

In-Core Instrument
Location

Reactor Vessel

Thermal Shield

Core Barrel

Surveillance Specimen
Holder Tube

Nuclear reactors contain fuel assemblies of fissionable material kept from going critical (exploding) by means of control rods containing materials called poisons *(boron, cadmium, hafnium or gadolinium) which regulate chain reactions. Worker (above left) inspects fuel stored at 3½-million-kilowatt Browns Ferry boiling water nuclear powerplant near Athens, Alabama.*

neutrons cause U-235 to fission more readily than do fast neutrons. Such thermal reactors utilize a core of some light element, such as hydrogen or deuterium or carbon, to reduce the kinetic energy of the neutrons. Hydrogen "moderators" are normally used in the form of water, hence the thermal reactor works best with a water coolant.

In 1962 the Light Water Reactor (LWR) became economically competitive with fossil-fuel electric generating plants, and today virtually all power reactors are of this type. There are two kinds of LWR reactors generally in use in this country — the Pressurized Water Reactor (PWR) and the Boiling Water Reactor (BWR). Both simply use the water coolant to make steam to run electric generators.

LWRs, while economically competitive with fossil fuel plants, have drawbacks — low fuel resource utilization, low thermal efficiency, high operating pressures, and high capital and fuel costs. By 1965 the unprecedented introduction of large numbers of commercial LWR units

Indian Point nuclear reactor of New York City's Consolidated Edison Company (upper left) is a first-generation plant, in operation since 1962. At right is Commonwealth Edison Company's Dresden nuclear plant near Morris, Ill., the world's first privately financed, full-scale nuclear plant. At lower left, California's San Onofre Nuclear Generating Station began operating in 1968. Nuclear plant at lower right supplies 420,000 kilowatts of electricity to Rochester, New York.

into the electric utility market resulted in growing public acceptance of nuclear power, particularly important in view of our necessity of independence from foreign energy sources. It was a tough selling job; people instinctively associated atomic power with explosive bombs.

Despite the hazards of radiation leakage, thermal pollution, and disposal of solid radioactive waste materials, LWRs, such as Consolidated Edison's Indian Point Station, Unit 1 in New York, in operation since 1962, have shown that a nuclear power plant can be operated safely and reliably as part of an electric generating system. The Indian Point reactor, generating some 275 megawatts of electricity, is called a first-generation nuclear plant. In this unit a pressurized water reactor supplies heat for steam generation, assisted by an oil-fired superheater.

In the United States, second-generation nuclear plants are water reactors of the pressurized water or boiling water types. Some supply up to 1200 megawatts of electricity per unit.

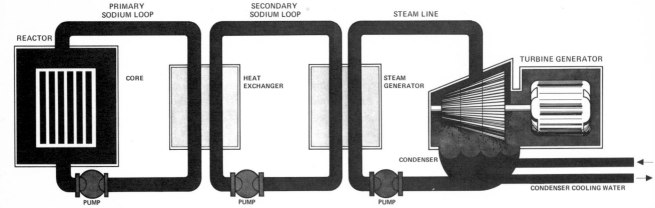

PRIMARY
SODIUM LOOP

SECONDARY
SODIUM LOOP

STEAM LINE

REACTOR

CORE

HEAT
EXCHANGER

STEAM
GENERATOR

TURBINE GENERATOR

CONDENSER

CONDENSER COOLING WATER

PUMP

PUMP

PUMP

The fast breeder reactor, America's highest-priority nuclear energy program, is cooled by liquid sodium, one of the best heat transfer mediums known. Like water-cooled reactors, breeders also produce heat by splitting atoms. Instead of U-235, breeders use plutonium 239 as their principal fuel. There is no "perpetual motion" involved— breeders economically utilize some 75% of the energy content of U-238, as against 2% potentially utilized in water-cooled reactors. In one year's operation, the fast breeder also produces 10% of the annual fissionable fuel requirement of a second breeder plant, thus extending the life of our limited uranium reserves by thousands of years. The first electricity ever generated from nuclear heat was producd at Idaho Falls in 1951, by a sodium-cooled fast breeder reactor, the EBR-1.

Currently, emphasis of the United States reactor development program is on the *Liquid Metal Fast Breeder Reactor* (LMFBR). In this reactor, liquid sodium is used instead of water as a coolant, and instead of ending up with radioactive waste materials, it "breeds" more fissionable fuel as a by-product, converting the uranium isotope U-238 into the fissionable isotope of another element — Plutonium-239.

Introduction of breeder reactors comes at a time when the world supply of Uranium 235, like fossil fuels, is limited. U. S. Atomic Energy Commission studies claim that this nation will require 206,000 tons of uranium oxide (U_3O_8) in the decade 1970-80 alone. Our own uranium reserves will fall short by 1,000,000 tons by 1985, says the AEC.

The chief advantage of the breeder reactor over the LWR type is that it can utilize the more plentiful uranium isotope *U-238* (99.3 percent of all uranium), converting it into fissionable plutonium, a miracle of transmutation that would have made the ancient alchemists turn green with envy and admiration.

USS Nautilus, first U.S. atomic-powered submarine, launched in 1954, outdid its Jules Verne namesake by traveling 62,500 miles without refueling on its maiden voyage. Admiral Hyman Rickover, father of the Navy's nuclear fleet, helped develop our first large-scale nuclear plant for producing electricity, at Shippingport, Pa.

It works this way: When a free neutron enters the nucleus of a U-238 atom, that atom becomes U-239, another uranium isotope. This atom is unstable, due to the new ratio of protons to neutrons, and seeks to stabilize itself. This happens spontaneously, when a neutron changes into a proton, releasing one electron with a surge of energy.

This transmutation process continues over a "half-life" of 23 minutes, the time required for half the amount of U-239 to decay into neptunium-239, changing from an element with a total of 92 protons + 147 neutrons to one with a total of 93 protons + 146 neutrons. It takes another 23 minutes for the rest of the material to change from uranium to neptunium, which is itself unstable. Within the next three days, the neptunium-239 will have become plutonium-239 (94 protons + 145 neutrons), a more stable isotope with a half-life of 24,360 years.

The AEC, in selling the country on breeder reactors, uses a poster that says: "Johnny had 3 truckloads of plutonium. He used 3 of them to

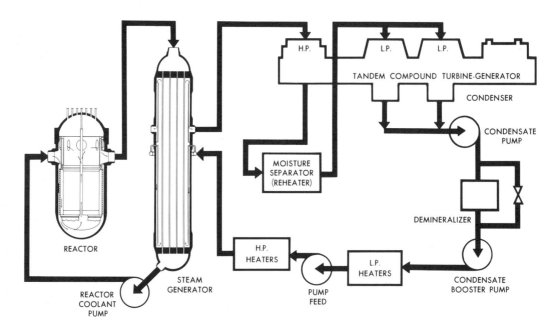

NUCLEAR PLANT CYCLE

Conventional nuclear power station is basically a heat source to generate steam to drive a turbine-generator, in a closed-loop arrangement whereby low-pressure (L.P.) and high-pressure (H.P.) heaters recycle steam. This is a Pressurized Water Reactor (PWR) system, forerunner of tomorrow's High Temperature Gas Reactor (HTGR) that utilizes thermal conversion and a fuel cycle of thorium-to-uranium 233.

light New York for 1 year. How much plutonium did Johnny have left? Answer — 4 truckloads."

Since 1966 a national energy program of high priority has been pursued to make fast breeders commercially operative by 1986. Another breeder reactor program, the High Temperature Gas Reactor (HTGR) is a helium-cooled, graphite-moderated thermal converter that utilizes a different fuel cycle — thorium-to-uranium 233 instead of U-238-to-plutonium 239. Since 1967 a 40,000,000-watt HTGR plant has been delivering power to the Philadelphia Electric Company from Peach Bottom, Pennsylvania, and in 1975 a 330,000,000-watt HTGR plant at Fort St. Vrain, Colorado, is scheduled to start operation. Gulf General Atomic, builder of the HTGR, hopes to install two more such plants in Pennsylvania, each with a capacity of 1,160,000,000 watts.

Along with a fossil-fuel shortage, the world may someday face a fresh-water shortage unless ways are found to convert sea water to fresh, economically on a large scale, using waste heat from nuclear power stations to run desalination plants. This plant at Freeport, Texas, converts 1,000,000 gallons of water daily by what is called the multiple-effect LTV (long-tube vertical) process.

And how will we use all this fantastic atomic power in the future? AEC believes a whole new economic and technological ball game will be played, one that may drastically change our way of life. First, ultra-high voltage transmission lines must be developed. New reactor cooling towers must be designed, to utilize waste heat from reactors that can be built safely inside urban areas.

Dual-purpose seashore high-temperature reactors will use waste heat to desalinate sea water, and so increase our supply of fresh water while producing power. Farm vehicles, road vehicles, and mass transit vehicles will switch from fossil fuels to electricity. All this can be achieved economically with introduction of the breeders — the potential savings of cheaper energy supply alone, over the remainder of this century, have been estimated at up to 2,000,000,000 dollars a year for each year large-scale introduction of breeders is advanced.

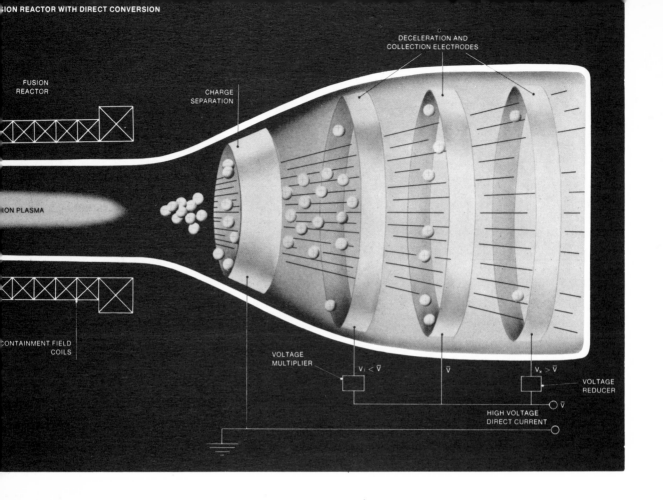

FUSION–
THE ULTIMATE ENERGY SOURCE

FUSION REACTORS, scientists agree, appear to hold the greatest hope for unlimited energy by the twenty-first century, for a number of valid reasons. The basic fuel, deuterium, exists in bountiful quantities in the seas, and extraction costs will be far less than that of electrical power generation. Further, environmental aspects of fusion power plants are favorable — there are only a few grams of fuel in a fusion reactor, and thus a nuclear explosion cannot occur. The only radioactive byproduct of the fuel cycle (tritium) can be recycled as fuel.

This ultimate energy source awaits final development of highly sophisticated atomic fusion devices called Controlled Thermonuclear Reactors (CTRs). The goal is to duplicate, in a practical manner, the vast energy release going on throughout the Universe, the result of collision and fusion of light hydrogen atoms under conditions of intense heat and extremely low pressure.

To understand the process of fusion, let's look at some basics of quantum mechanics — in essence, what goes on inside the world of the atom. We know, to begin with, that there are four states of matter — solid, liquid, gas, and *plasma.* The first three are familiar to us, on and near the Earth's surface. The fourth constitutes the Earth's upper ionized atmosphere and more than 99 percent of all other matter in the Universe.

Alchemists had a reasonable intellectual grasp of this when they divided all matter into four basic "elements" — Earth, water, air, and fire. Plasma is a state achieved by further heating up a gas, so that its constituent atomic parts — the electrons and nuclei — can break free of each other. Free nuclei are called *ions,* and the breakup process is called *ionization.* Hydrogen ionization occurs at a temperature of about 10,000°C, relatively low compared to the 100,000,000°C required for fusion.

Natural plasmas occur rarely in our environment—in lightning strokes and in auroras—for example. Elsewhere in the Universe the plasma state is the most common form of matter. Stars like our Sun are giant fusion reactors, and the space around them is filled with dilute plasmas of extremely low density.

In the plasma state, molecules and atoms of ordinary matter, by nature electrically neutral, break down into positively charged ions and negatively charged electrons. Under favorable conditions positive ions, formed from light elements such as hydrogen, may fuse, creating a more complex nucleus. In this process they lose a fraction of their mass, which is converted into energy.

The Sun's interior is composed of a dense, hot, hydrogen plasma, its ions slowly and continually fusing with an enormous energy release. An analogous reaction takes place, but very rapidly, in a hydrogen bomb. The CTR (Controlled Thermonuclear Reactor) program seeks to control the fusion of ions in a rarefied plasma of *deuterium,* or of *deuterium* and *tritium.*

DEUTERIUM NUCLEUS

Both deuterium and tritium are isotopes of ordinary hydrogen (H). Deuterium has twice the mass of hydrogen, and tritium three times its mass. Deuterium is so abundant it could supply the Earth's total energy needs for *one billion years.* Tritium may be manufactured from lithium, another abundant element. Unlike fission fuels — uranium, thorium, and plutonium — deuterium and tritium release no dangerous radioactive waste products when they fuse.

TRITIUM NUCLEUS

Where a hydrogen atom consists of a single electron revolving around a much heavier nucleus (the proton), an atom of deuterium consists of an electron revolving around a nucleus of one proton and one neutron. Similarly, an atom of tritium consists of an electron revolving around a nucleus of a proton and two neutrons. All three atoms have positively charged nuclei, equal in magnitude to their negatively charged electrons.

HELIUM NUCLEUS

The first successful thermonuclear reaction on Earth took place in 1952 at Elugelab Reef in the South Pacific, with explosion of history's first hydrogen bomb. Controlled thermonuclear reactors (CTRs) do not contain fuel enough for an explosion.

Fusion of two nuclei is normally opposed, because their positive charges repel each other, unless, by super-heating, their energies of motion are high enough to overcome the natural electrical repulsion. Deuterium and tritium fuse more readily than other combinations of nuclei, hence fusion reactor designs are generally based on this fuel process.

The minimum energy of motion required to induce a deuterium-tritium fusion is about 10,000 electron volts. (The energy gained by an electron's acceleration through a potential difference of 10,000 volts.) Such an energy level can be attained in two ways—by using a 10,000-volt electron accelerator, or by heating particles to 100,000,000°C. In a hydrogen bomb, such a heat is attained by atomic *fission,* before fusion can occur with its thousand-fold energy release.

The first successful thermonuclear reaction on Earth took place November 1, 1952, on the Elugelab Reef in the South Pacific, when a Hiroshima-type atom bomb was detonated to produce "solar" temperatures and pressures in which fusion could take place. The results was the first hydrogen bomb explosion in history.

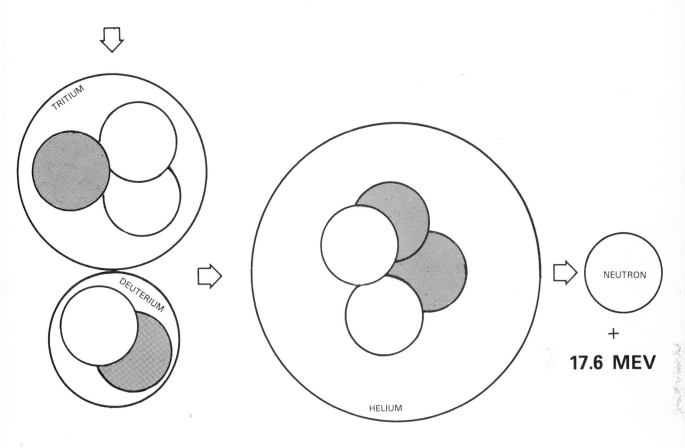

The deuterium-tritium fusion reaction yields one helium nucleus, a neutron, and 17,600,000 electron volts of energy, roughly a thousand times the energy input of 10,000 electron volts. To attain such a reaction, and to control it as a self-sustaining, or chain reaction, has presented almost insurmountable technical challenges, now being overcome in the laboratory. What is needed to achieve controlled fusion can be attained by creating a deuterium-tritium plasma at a density of about 1/100,000th of that of the air around us, and confining it within a fixed volume for about one second at a temperature of 100,000,000°C.

Plasma produced in a fusion reactor on Earth, however, cannot be confined long enough for fusion to take place within walls made of ordinary solid matter — contact with the walls would immediately cool the plasma below the required heat level. In the Sun, plasmas are confined by gigantic magnetic fields.

Spacecraft such as Pioneer V revealed more knowledge of the solar

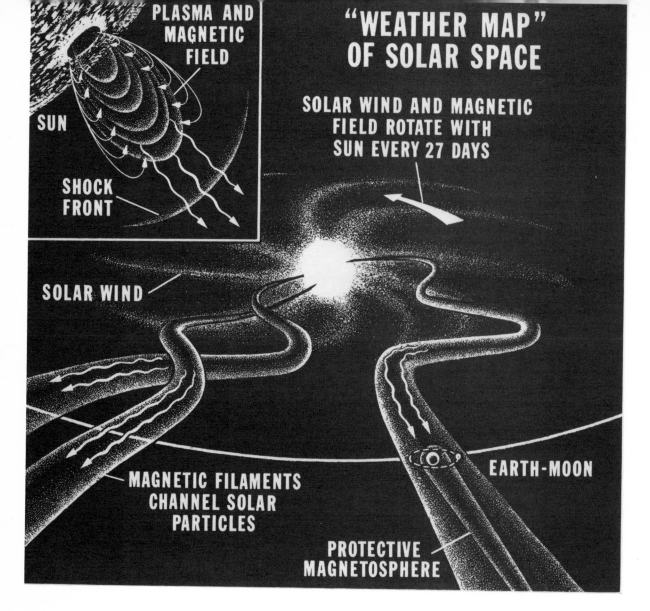

PLASMA AND MAGNETIC FIELD

"WEATHER MAP" OF SOLAR SPACE

SOLAR WIND AND MAGNETIC FIELD ROTATE WITH SUN EVERY 27 DAYS

SUN

SHOCK FRONT

SOLAR WIND

MAGNETIC FILAMENTS CHANNEL SOLAR PARTICLES

EARTH-MOON

PROTECTIVE MAGNETOSPHERE

fusion process, wherein lay the key to successful CTR design. These satellites investigated giant solar winds originating in the Sun's corona. (The source of the Sun's energy, hydrogen fusion, consumes 657 million tons of hydrogen a second.) Solar winds flow outward in twisted paths, channeled by intertwined magnetic fields generated from fantastically strong electric currents associated with sunspots.

Early efforts to duplicate this process on Earth led to the design of a device called a *racetrack stellerator*. Hot plasma particles were confined by magnetic lines of force, produced by external coils that followed a twisting path, like a corkscrew wrapped around a doughnut, or *torus*.

The stellerator was a step toward design and development of a satisfactory "magnetic bottle" needed to prevent plasma particles from escaping in a direction along the magnetic field lines. Two solutions to this problem presented themselves — an open-ended magnetic bottle, with field strengths strong enough at both ends to contain the plasma (called a *mirror*

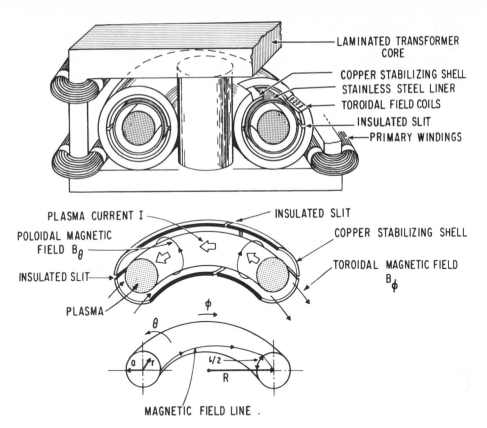

LAMINATED TRANSFORMER CORE
COPPER STABILIZING SHELL
STAINLESS STEEL LINER
TOROIDAL FIELD COILS
INSULATED SLIT
PRIMARY WINDINGS

PLASMA CURRENT I
POLOIDAL MAGNETIC FIELD B_θ
INSULATED SLIT
PLASMA
INSULATED SLIT
COPPER STABILIZING SHELL
TOROIDAL MAGNETIC FIELD B_ϕ
MAGNETIC FIELD LINE.

Soviet scientists at Moscow's Kurchatov Institute developed a device called a Tokamak, to learn how to duplicate solar fusion on Earth. A strong toroidal magnetic field is set up by external coils, and a current is induced in a plasma torus (doughnut) by a large iron-core transformer. The plasma current completes the magnetic bottle with a magnetic field component, also heats the plasma much like an electric toaster.

machine), or a closed toroidal (doughnut-shaped) magnetic bottle. Another way to achieve fusion is now under study—by freely exploding plasmas not confined by a magnetic bottle, providing the plasma is sufficiently dense. Recent development of high-powered lasers (*light amplification by stimulated emission of radiation*) have made this method technologically feasible.

The most promising fusion device now seems to be the Adiabatic Toroidal Compressor (ATC)—a doughnut-shaped magnetic bottle in which the heating cycle starts with an intense electric current flowing through a plasma inside the doughnut. This type of heating was originated by Soviet scientists at the Kurchatov Institute in Moscow.

What was needed next was some way to confine a hot plasma for a sufficient time—about one second—for fusion to take place. The answer seemed to lie in using extreme temperatures, roughly equivalent to those inside the Sun. But can we attain them?

ADIABATIC TOROIDAL COMPRESSOR
(ATC)

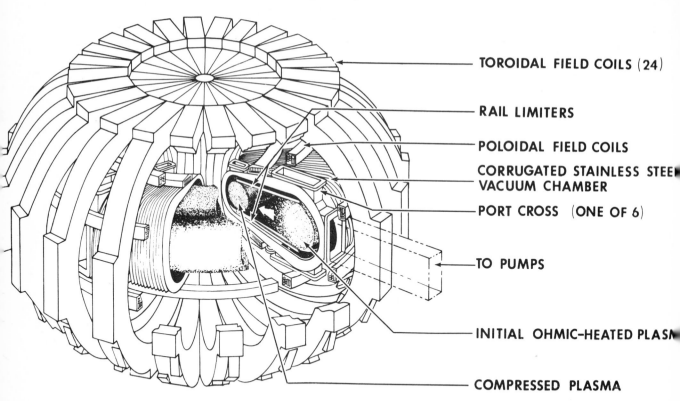

TOROIDAL FIELD COILS (24)

RAIL LIMITERS

POLOIDAL FIELD COILS

CORRUGATED STAINLESS STEEL
VACUUM CHAMBER

PORT CROSS (ONE OF 6)

TO PUMPS

INITIAL OHMIC-HEATED PLASMA

COMPRESSED PLASMA

Princeton University's Plasma Physics Laboratory improved on the Russian Tokamak in their Adiabatic Toroidal Compressor, by inducing plasma current with air-core transformer coils, allowing substantial compression and plasma heating within the plasma doughnut. Plasma compression is achieved by a pulsed vertical magnetic field.

An exciting breakthrough was made by the Russians with their fusion research device, called a *T-3 Tokamak*. This device could contain a plasma sufficiently large to permit electron temperatures above 10,000,000°C, achieved by passing a current of electricity through the plasma. Further heating could then be accomplished in different ways — by compressing the plasma, by subjecting the plasma to a pumping action in the magnetic field, or by other methods now under study. Once fusion was ignited, the hot plasma would continue to supply its own heat for igniting newly injected fuel.

In 1970 the Soviet tokamak experiments were confirmed at Princeton University's Plasma Physics Laboratory, one of several engaged in a multi-million dollar fusion research program throughout the United States. Princeton's Adiabatic Toroidal Compressor (ATC), developed by Dr. Harold P. Furth, is the first tokamak device to achieve an electron density range in which such fusion reactors will eventually operate.

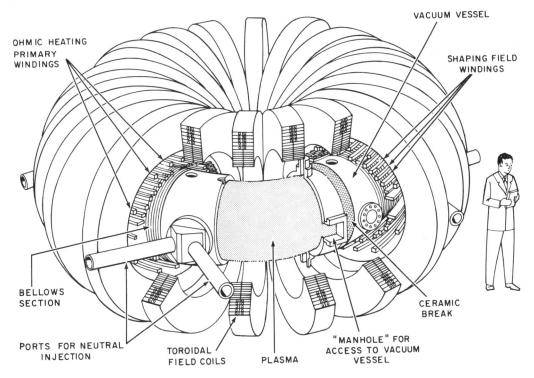

OHMIC HEATING
PRIMARY
WINDINGS

VACUUM VESSEL

SHAPING FIELD
WINDINGS

BELLOWS
SECTION

CERAMIC
BREAK

PORTS FOR NEUTRAL
INJECTION

TOROIDAL
FIELD COILS

PLASMA

"MANHOLE" FOR
ACCESS TO VACUUM
VESSEL

Scheduled for operation in July 1975 is the Princeton Large Torus (PLT), a research device of intermediate size designed to prove out the theory that the bigger the plasma ring, the longer the plasma confinement time. To achieve fusion ignition, a plasma must be contained for about one second.

While the ATC's plasma ion temperature reaches about 7,000,000°C, this is significantly high enough to show that a full-sized ATC fusion reactor can reach the 100,000,000°C needed to achieve deuterium-tritium ignition.

The Princeton Plasma Physics Laboratory team, headed by Dr. Melvin B. Gottlieb, has made a number of improvements on the Soviet tokamak technology. A massive copper shell, first thought necessary for plasma stabilization, has been replaced by electronically controlled magnet coils, and the Russian-type large iron-core transformer, used to induce the heating current in the tokamak plasma, has been replaced by a smaller air-core transformer. By eliminating the copper shell and the iron core transformer, another major breakthrough was achieved — the ATC now can compress the tokamak plasma sufficiently for the electric and ion temperatures to shoot up by a factor of three, and the electron density up by a factor of five.

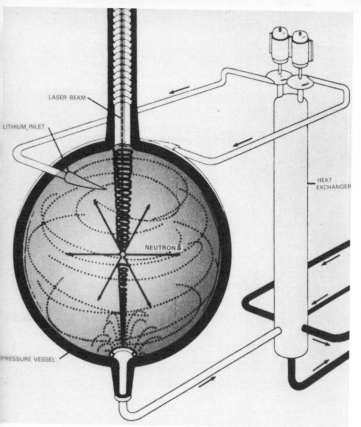

A laser beam 1,000,000 times brighter than the Sun mig be used to ignite fusion reaction without the need for magnetic bottle, focusing it on frozen deuterium pelle

Controlled fusion was demonstrated in March, 1972, at a fusion test reactor called Scyllac, at the Los Alamos Scientific Laboratory. Ion temperatures in a 16½-foot arc-shaped magnetic bottle reached 10,000,000°C for the 10 microseconds.

At the Lawrence Radiation Laboratory (LRL) in Livermore, California, further progress is being made toward controlled thermonuclear fusion. A device there called the 2X Experiment, using what is called a *"magnetic well,"* has stabilized plasma confinement dramatically — in this experiment, a plasma burst is injected, trapped, and heated by *magnetic compression.*

Also at LRL, a way has been found to attain tremendous energy release through proton-*fissioning* of the isotope boron-11, the most common form of that element. Boron-11 fission products are three non-radioactive, electrically charged particles (helium nuclei). This experiment holds promise for future nuclear fission reactors with 100,000 times fewer radioactive byproducts than existing uranium power plants. Besides, boron-11 is virtually inexhaustible, as it occurs abundantly in the oceans and in dry lakebeds as borax.

Fusion energy conversion is a simple process — the heat is absorbed in a thick lithium salt blanket which surrounds the fusion chamber, and is removed by a heat exchanger for use in a conventional steam electric plant. Neutrons released by fusion ultimately enter into other nuclear reactions with the lithium, to generate tritium, which is separated and fed back into the reactor as fuel.

72

Nation's first pressurized water reactor/simulator.

What remains to be done to make fusion energy commercially feasible is basically to build a full-size reactor patterned after today's laboratory devices, and resolve the final operational technologies. Once ignited, a fusion reactor will operate on a small scale as a manmade "Sun," and as in the Sun, the byproduct of hydrogen isotope fusion is energy plus helium, a harmless inert gas.

For the young men and women of America, who will enter adulthood in the next two generations, power from fusion reactors will open a whole new world. Even today's youth are finding a place in this exciting new technology, learning to become nuclear powerplant operators by practicing reactor manipulation in modern simulators, where a mistake is simply a learning experience, not a disaster!

Is there still another energy source beyond fusion? The possibility has been raised, and partly verified in the laboratory, that distant parts of the Universe may be composed of *antimatter*, equal in total amount to ordinary matter. In 1930, while describing wavelike properties of the electron, P. A. M. Dirac at Cambridge University arrived at an equation consistent with observed behavior of the electron except for one flaw—electrons could exist with the electrical charges reversed.

Atoms of reverse charges have since been produced—antiprotons and antineutrons were discovered with the Berkeley bevatron particle accelerator—and the implication is that matter exists in which everything is reversed, including time. A collison of matter and antimatter results

World's largest magnetohydrodynamic (MHD) generator, built in 1960's to power an Air Force wind tunnel to test reentry space vehicles, is now in use for government research into MHD technology as electrical power source for tomorrow. A 5000°F exhaust, like a rocket engine's, blasts through a 500-ton magnet, producing a high mass energy flow equal to that of a 30,000-pound thrust rocket.

in mutual annihilation, and all that is left is — *energy.* However, any hope for significant anti-matter energy generation on Earth is far-fetched.

To sum it all up, in the long view, no real energy shortage exists in the world today. Rather, the power available to run society's machine is sufficient to last for possibly millions of years, if we but choose to order our priorities intelligently. The full transfer to nuclear energy will take time, and it is perhaps fortunate that the energy crisis of the mid-1970's came when it did. We now know that fossil fuels stored in Spaceship Earth must be reserved for emergency use only, and that the answer to the worldwide energy problem lies in drawing on those same sources that have kept the Universe running since the beginnings of time—the energies within the atom itself.

MHD power conversion, combined with a high temperature fission or fusion reactor, could be the ultimate power plant of the future, in terms of compactness, efficiency low maintenance, and minimum thermal pollution. Richard J. Rosa, chief scientist of AVCO Everett Research Laboratory's MHD Project, in 1959 successfully lit a bank of light bulbs with history's first MHD generator, the Mark I (above). A MHD generator has no moving parts—it produces electric power simply by expanding super-hot gas through a magnetic field. Russia already uses a MHD generator to light the streets of Moscow.

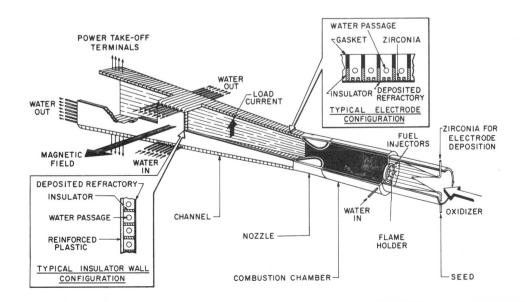

E.O.S. GEOMAGNETIC THRUSTOR
USING ION PLASMA CONTACTS FOR LUNAR SHUTTLE

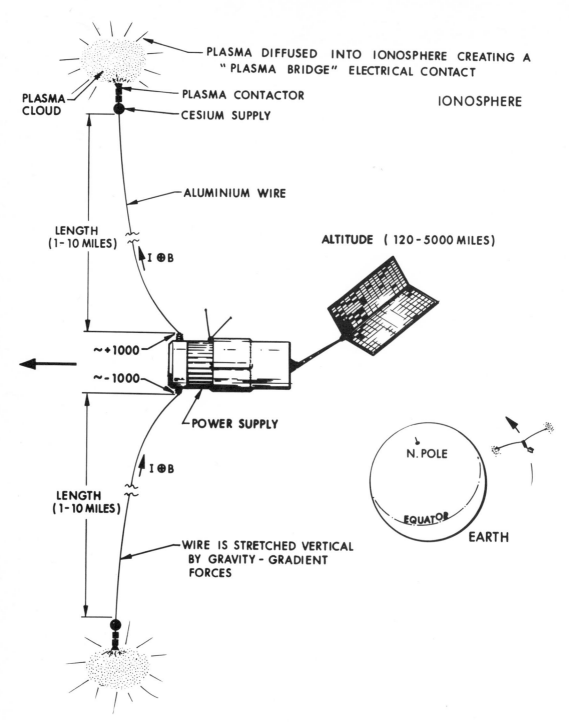

PLASMA DIFFUSED INTO IONOSPHERE CREATING A "PLASMA BRIDGE" ELECTRICAL CONTACT

PLASMA CLOUD

PLASMA CONTACTOR

CESIUM SUPPLY

IONOSPHERE

ALUMINIUM WIRE

ALTITUDE (120 - 5000 MILES)

LENGTH (1 - 10 MILES)

I ⊕ B

~ +1000

~ -1000

POWER SUPPLY

LENGTH (1 - 10 MILES)

I ⊕ B

WIRE IS STRETCHED VERTICAL BY GRAVITY - GRADIENT FORCES

N. POLE

EQUATOR

EARTH

Unusual proposal to power lunar shuttle vehicle by tapping the Earth's magnetic field. Key to its operation would be two plasma clouds suspended at ends of pair of 10-mile long wires, to make efficient contact with the ionospheric plasma. Device is called a geomagnetic thrustor.

GLOSSARY

ADIABATIC TOROIDAL COMPRESSOR—A laboratory device holding great promise of realizing thermonuclear fusion power, by heating a deuterium-tritium plasma in a doughnut-shaped magnetic bottle.

ANTI-MATTER—Matter composed of the counterparts of ordinary matter; antiprotons instead of protons, positrons instead of electrons, antineutrons instead of neutrons.

BREEDER REACTOR—A fission reactor that utilizes the more plentiful isotope Uranium-238, converting it into fissionable Plutonium-239.

BRITISH THERMAL UNIT—Heat required to raise the temperature of one pound of water one degree Fahrenheit at 39.2°F.

COSMIC RAYS—Streams of high-energy radiation from unknown sources in space.

CTRS—Atomic fusion devices called Controlled Thermonuclear Reactors, of far greater energy potential than fission reactors.

DEUTERIUM—A hydrogen isotope with twice the mass of ordinary hydrogen, sometimes called heavy hydrogen.

$E = mc^2$—Einstein's classic equation, in which total energy in mass equals mass times the square of the velocity of light.

ELECTRON—A subatomic particle consisting of a charge of negative electricity.

ENTROPY—Degradation of matter and energy in the Universe to an ultimate state of inert uniformity.

FISSION—The splitting of an atomic nucleus with a vast release of energy.

FUSION—The union of certain light elements, forming nuclei of heavier elements with enormous energy release.

GASEOUS DIFFUSION PLANT—A device for separating uranium isotopes U-235 from U-238, by passing them through fine membranes in the form of uranium hexafluoride gas.

GEOTHERMAL ENERGY—Energy from radioactivity of the Earth's internal core, released in the form of heat.

IONS—Free atomic nuclei that make up a plasma.

ISOTOPE—A variation of a chemical element with a different atomic mass.

LASER—A light beam intensified by stimulating natural oscillations of atoms.

MEGAWATT—One million watts.

MHD—Magnetohydrodynamics, the study of electrically conductive plasmas in the presence of a magnetic field.

NEUTRON—An uncharged atomic particle, equal in mass to a proton.

PLASMA—The fourth state of matter, after solid, liquid, and gaseous.

PROTON—An atomic particle identical with the nucleus of a hydrogen atom.

QUANTUM MECHANICS—General mathematical theory dealing with observable interactions of matter and radiation.

RADIOACTIVITY—Spontaneous emission of alpha, beta, or gamma rays by disintegration of atomic nuclei.

SOLAR WIND—Outpouring of plasma from the Sun.

TOKAMAK—A Russian fusion experiment for heating a plasma inside a torus.

TORUS—A doughnut-shaped device, sometimes used to contain a plasma for fusion.

TRITIUM—A radioactive hydrogen isotope with a nucleus three times the mass of ordinary hydrogen.

WALL EFFECT—The cooling effect of a plasma coming into contact with a container, avoidable by using so-called magnetic bottles.

PICTURE CREDITS

Atomic Energy Commission
    29, 55, 58-A & B, 59-A, B & D
Atomic Energy Commission of Canada, Ltd.
    56, 57
American Gas Association
    15, 31
The Anaconda Co.
    30
American Petroleum Institute
    11-A, 12, 13
Avco Everett Research Laboratory
    75-A & B
Babcock & Wilcox
    22, 32-A, 33-A & B, 37, 58-C, 72
Billings Energy Research Corp.
    28-D
Don Dwiggins
    11-B, 28-C, 40, 65
Drake Well Museum
    25
Electro-Optical Systems, Inc.
    76
Grumman Aerospace Corp.
    44
Gulf Energy & Environmental Systems
    62
High Altitude Observatory, Boulder, Colo.
    49
Hughes Tool Co.
    10-B
Institute of Aeronautical Sciences
    26-B
Las Vegas News Bureau
    34

Livermore Research Laboratory
    72
Los Alamos Scientific Laboratory
    54
Mount Wilson & Palomar Observatories
    43, 45, 47, 50, 51
National Aeronautics and Space Administration
    Front Cover, pp. 7, 32-B, 46, 68
Pacific Gas & Electric Co.
    39
Phototheque EDF
    36
Princeton University Plasma Physics Laboratory
    64, 69, 70, 71
Salt River Valley Project
    17, 18
Shell Oil Co.
    10-A
The Singer Co.
    73
Southern California Edison Co.
    Back Cover, pp. 14, 35, 38, 41, 52, 59-C, 60
Security Pacific National Bank Historical Collection
    20
UCLA Research Library
    19, 2-A & B, 23, 24, 26-A, C & D,
    28-A & B, 32-C, 42
United States Army Signal Corps
    27
United States Air Force
    48, 66, 74
United States Department of the Interior
    16, 63, 67
United States Navy
    61

INDEX

"Exploding across the land with the shock wave of an atomic bomb, the worldwide energy crisis of 1973–74 caught millions of people unawares. In the United States, as in other countries, certain facts stood out. For too long we had run our cars, heated and lighted our homes, and run our factories on precious, limited supplies of fossil fuels—the natural gas, oil, coal and shale deposits stored in the Earth for hundreds of millions of years. The answer to the problem was plain—the world must eventually turn to other energy sources and lock up this planet's remaining fossil fuels in a treasure vault marked *For Emergency Use Only!*"

In this absorbing and challenging book author Don Dwiggins explores these other energy sources, explaining exactly what they are, how they work, and what potentials they hold for the future of mankind. Beginning with a brief outline of the steps man has taken in his eternal quest for power down through the ages, the author discusses present and future possibilities in such prime energy sources as direct and indirect solar energy, tidal and geothermal energy, then goes on to consider cosmic energy—the splitting of the atom for power, and, lastly, controlled atomic fusion which, scientists believe, holds the greatest future promise for unlimited energy upon this earth. In gathering his material Mr. Dwiggins went to primary sources for information, interrogating top authorities in their special fields. The result is a lucid, comprehensive and intensely interesting survey of a subject which is of crucial importance to us all. Dozens of dynamic photographs and clear explanatory diagrams illuminate the text.

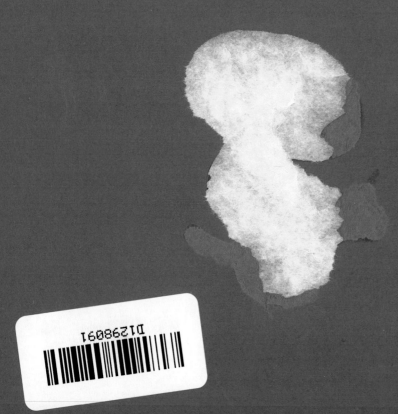